Note

7/29/2014

Dear, dear Frank —

Lots of love,
Nancy

Notes From the Other Side

Lynn Scott, Spirit Intuitive

2008

Booksurge Publishing

Visit www.Amazon.com to order additional copies

Notes From the Other Side

For my husband Bob.
The love of my life.

CONTENTS

Preface

NOTES FROM THE OTHER SIDE endeavors to provide inspiring information for those on *this* side of the veil, from heartfelt individuals on *the other side* wishing to share their stories.

As a spirit intuitive, I act as a conduit for those in spirit wishing to communicate. In many ways it's similar to the work of an interpreter: hearing information in one form, translating it into another, all the while attempting to maintain the integrity of the original communication.

The reason I mention this is because while each story is unique, you may notice a similar tone throughout the book which is, admittedly, my own: the intuitive translator. That noted, I assure you the journeys described belong to those who lived them*.

What awaits us in the afterlife, I believe, is directly determined by our choices in this life. As a Christian, I have faith the best and brightest life on both sides of the veil comes through Jesus Christ.

Because of my faith, it comes as no real surprise that the majority of those wishing to share their stories with me also share my beliefs. However, this book is by no means limited to only those beliefs. As you will find, when a person with a heart of gold dies and comes "home," it is always an occasion for celebration in the afterlife.

* For reasons of privacy many of the names described herein have been changed.

Introduction

Have you ever been inspired to do something you've never considered before? In what still seems like a bolt out of the blue, a strong desire came over me one day to begin intuiting stories from people who died, yet wish to communicate their unique wisdom regarding life from the perspective of the afterlife.

With what felt like God's hand guiding me, the stories came pouring out. While the majority are comforting, a few are not until the person comes to terms with their conscience and a place of peace with God. Ultimately, each describes their life lessons through the lens of true gratitude.

I offer these accounts to be true, but ultimately you decide. Either way, please know if they even *feel* possible, then the miracle for your heart is real.

NED

Tough day at work. Mail everywhere was stacked on my desk plus appointments had filled in all week long. No wonder I was tired. *No rest for the weary*, I thought, but then remembered my work ethic to never forget how hard my parents had worked to send me to college so I could become somebody. I chose to become a CPA.

Trouble rarely occurred at work. I took great care with each client to be certain they knew their risks if they cut corners with their bookkeeping and taxes. Even so, when faced with the barrel of a shotgun, I knew work hadn't prepared me for that.

Stopping here for a moment is important to me because I need you to know I hadn't taken seriously a letter I read earlier that day warning me of my impending death.

But back to the barrel of the shotgun: Never had I held a shotgun or seen one before, so looking down the long nose of one was completely paralyzing to me. Somehow, though, I thought to talk calmly with my client whom I had supposedly ruined with my financial advice regarding his taxes. He warned me to shut up, I'd already given him enough bad advice over the years, and to sit back down.

He's mentally unhinged, I remember thinking as I saw his eyes widen while he looked at his watch over and over again. *Is he waiting for something?* Just then my desk phone rang. He ordered me to answer it and said it was my one opportunity to save myself.

Pushing a prepared letter before me, I saw he had scripted what he needed me to say to his banker in Hong Kong. Laughing a little, he said, "Let's see if you can get *this* right." So I answered the phone trying to sound normal, but bit my tongue trying not to say anything dumb.

After the call ended and his banker heard what he needed to hear in order to prepare a large loan to my client, I breathed a heavy sigh of relief but then realized by the look in his eyes this ordeal wasn't over.

I called to his attention that the people in the office next door often pop in without notice. He locked the door. So now I had a decision to make: Sit there until he does something, or do something myself.

At last I coughed so loud it caught him off guard. I rushed him but he was ready. I heard the shout of my own voice yelling, "No!" as the shell casing flew out and the shot pierced my heart.

Coming to wasn't easy. I had fallen to the floor with such force it alone knocked the wind out of me. But within about a minute (as far as I could tell), I came free from my body, stood next to it and saw it was ravaged with blood and shrapnel. Blood was everywhere, but he was gone. Before hurrying out after my collapse, he stole my wallet and took back the letter he had scripted. *Nowhere to go*, I remember thinking. *Is this what death is like? You just exit your body and...*

Just as I was contemplating my choices, I felt a deep, deep stirring from within to *listen very carefully*. It wasn't like a warning, but it was a stern voice nonetheless. With those firm words of advice, I came to even more. But in order to listen more carefully, I focused on the floor where I stood and tried not to think about anything else.

My back, which had always ached, was fine, I suddenly noticed. In fact, it continued to feel better and better the more I focused on the floor. *How could this be?* I questioned myself.

"Why are you so surprised?" I heard from within. This sudden pop-in voice confounded me, but soon I refocused on the floor and thought about the question.

"Well," I silently answered back, "how can I be feeling better after such severe injuries?"

"Nothing is impossible," I heard. "You came free from your mortal body, returning back into your light body–your *real* body."

Yes, I recall thinking. *This is my real body*. It felt more natural and real. "But what happens next? That's me there, too, lying on the floor in all that blood."

"That *was* you," the voice said. "But because you prepared for death one day long ago by asking for protection, I have been with you knowing this day would come." The voice continued, "You are first and always yourself, Ned. But you're not always your mortal self."

I had to think about this. If I'm always Ned, but not always in the body, then who is Ned not in the body?

"I'm so glad you asked," I heard. "You are me and I am you, but I am the eternal Ned. The one without fear or worries about what tomorrow may bring. I am you with all the freedom in the world!"

"It's good to meet you, I guess," I stammered out. "Where have you been all my life?"

"Nowhere until you asked for protection that day. That is when you created me as your God-force from within to come forward and lead you. Before, I was dormant. Like a seed to a flower without water, soil or sunlight for it to burst forward into life."

"Am I hallucinating?" I asked, still unsure of what was happening and unfolding. "Am I mentally ill?"

"Some might say you are, but do you feel you are?" the voice asked back.

"No. In fact, like my back, I'm feeling better and better."

"Good. That's the way it's supposed to happen."

With that I felt a little better, but still wondered about the fate of my body. "What's going to happen with that?" I asked pointing to my body on the floor.

"Your wife will have to come to terms with your death. An investigation will take place and a funeral will complete the necessities for your body."

My wife, I thought sympathetically. *She is strong when she has to be, but her upbringing was hard and she's always needed me.*

"Your wife will still need you, Ned," I heard. "In fact, she will need you now more than ever. Her heart will hurt for a long time. But if you believe in the God who created us, Jesus, you can come back and become her Earthly guide."

"Really?" I blurted out, "I knew people sometimes pretended their loved ones were still with them after death, but I thought it only wishful thinking."

"No, Ned. It's God's grace keeping loved ones together, even after one completes their mortal life. If they feel compelled to be together, God offers them the chance to come back and become an unseen guide, an angel, as some might say."

"What if they don't want to come back? Where do they go then?"

"They come home to be with Jesus, but only in time. That's what the Second Coming is about. They slumber just as you have at night. And when Jesus calls their name, they awaken, and Jesus resurrects them. Together with all their loved ones, they come home."

Before I could say or think about anything more, I knew with all my heart I wanted to come back and become a useful guide for my wife. "What should I do next?" I asked the voice within.

"Smile first," I heard.

"Smile?" What a strange thing to have me do, on this day of my death.

"No, Ned. This is the day you are reborn. You were a wonderful man who worked hard to do well for your family. You are being rewarded today for your efforts in trying to help your family and those less fortunate. Blessings are coming upon you even now. Can you feel them?"

"I can!" Indeed, I felt a sudden turnaround of events. I felt this wonderful golden opportunity whereas just moments before I had felt lost.

"So now it's you and me," the voice said. "We are one. The light and the shadow. The yin and the yang. You've come full circle to find yourself, and you've welcomed yourself home. Good job, Ned. Life is good."

No truer words have ever been spoken, I recall thinking. *No truer words.* Then suddenly, without warning, I was back in my bed with my wife, only she was ill or sick or something. I could tell by looking at her she had nothing in her eyes as she lay there. Nothing. Lying beside her I could eventually hear her thoughts as she spoke my name over and over, "Ned. Oh, Ned. Where are you? I need you so much. I'm lost without you."

I felt her heartbeat in mine. Truly. Even though my mortal body was deceased, the rhythm of my heart was still alive.

"I'm right here," I said tenderly as I pressed my hand into hers. "I won't leave you. I promise. You've given me so much. Now it's my turn to give back to you, my precious."

She looked wide awake now but still seemed dazed. "Lost," she had said. That's when I recalled saying how I was lost and my eternal self came to save me.

"Listen to me," I ordered her with some authority, "you have to want to live. I will not just let you wither-up and die. It's not your time. But it is my time to be your protector. Let me do that. But first you have to want to live for me to get to still be with you, otherwise there's no work for me to do and I'll have to go away until it's your time to cross over."

"Company's coming," I heard her say to herself. "I need to get up and get ready."

"Yes!" I enthusiastically agreed. *Get up and get prepared for life! Company is coming!*

(pause)

Invitations are often sent out to those who cross over ahead of their loved ones. These invitations are more special than you know, dear reader, because they allow those of us on this side to stay with you on your side.

But you have to do your part. You have to want us to be with you. You have to want life. To watch you wither away would nearly kill us all over again. That's when God calls our names and returns us back to the other side where we plan in our sleep what our life back together will be like someday.

Stay awake! Stay in-tuned with your eternal self. Ask it to become your voice of reason. You'll be amazed how different that voice will be–less driven by fear or worries.

It's taken me a long time to be able to come through to someone who wants to hear my story. It's unremarkable in many ways to those of us on this side, but I know from experience it's a truly remarkable journey to those of you on your side.

Know I'll be here to meet and greet you, whoever you are, if someday you want to meet in person. I know I'm looking forward to that day!

ERICA

A long time ago when I was only fourteen years old, I went out looking for mushrooms with my grandparents. They were experts at it so we often ate them as we wandered in the woods.

It was a beautiful day. I remember because I saw Grandma coughing a lot which wasn't like her, especially on sunny days. But as we kept going I noticed something new in her eyes, a look of concern and maybe even fear.

Grandpa knew something, I could tell. He kept quiet but also kept looking at her while wiping his nose. *Why aren't they talking to me*, I thought. *They're unusually quiet today. It must be something they can't talk about,* I recall thinking.

After our outing was over and we were back at my house, Grandpa came outside and put his arm around me. "Grandma's not well," he said tenderly. "I know you know it, but I had to get her permission to talk with you about it, first."

Presented with news like this was unreal. It's not like you can say or do something that will cause a change. *Wait a minute*, I thought. *It's not like she is dying in the house right now. Maybe this is just the beginning of something that can be treated.*

I guess I looked at Grandpa with eyes that spoke my wish, because he said what she had was terminal and could not be treated. He lowered his head saying it had been each of their wish to die together, but it looked like it wouldn't work out that way.

How we die (the way we *wish* it would happen) I later learned is valuable and important. So while Grandpa thought it was inevitable Grandma would die first, it didn't turn out that way.

Later that night while reading in my room, the phone rang. It was Grandma. "Something's wrong with Grandpa," she told Mom. "He's not responding to my touch or words. Please help," she pleaded.

He's not responding to her touch or words? That was nothing like Grandpa. He loves her touch and always listens to her. This must be serious.

After Dad came back with Mom from Grandma's house, they immediately took me by the shoulders and explained it must have been Grandpa's time to go. He had a stroke and wasn't able to hold on at all, not even in time for the paramedics.

They said Grandma was in shock and couldn't speak. She sighed a lot, they noticed, but couldn't get her to say what she was thinking or needing.

Mom told me most of the time Grandma just kept looking off in the distance as if something were there. There was. Later I found out it was Grandpa, saying his final goodbye to her as he softly dissipated from their house. Her heart, I now know, went with him.

Nine months later to the day Grandma died while rubbing down her favorite cat, Angel. He was special, Grandpa told me years before, because he could sense things most people couldn't. Grandpa wanted Grandma to have an angel to watch over her, and Angel did.

Not long after Grandma died, Angel did, too. The cat was warm when it died, unlike most older cats, because I think it still got rub downs from Grandma even though she wasn't there in the flesh.

Sometime later when my parents got back to their normal routine, I heard them talking about what to do with Grandma's things. Most of her belongings were valuable to Grandma, they agreed, but not worth much to anyone else.

It was too much to bear. Grandma and Grandpa's things getting thrown out. *Wasn't there a place where we could store their things for me someday?* I secretly wished.

Eleven years later I rode the monorail in Seattle at the World's Fair. It was a gas! I didn't think anyone, anywhere, could possibly be having as an exhilarating experience as I was.

Incredibly, as it sped on its tracks I heard in my head Grandma telling me she saved many of those things for me, and not to feel bad about them being tossed out. She said if you treasure something it's always there for you. Someday, she insisted, you'll see!

That was the treasure, I thought, *hearing from Grandma again!* Her voice–ringing in my inner ears like a phone with just one thin wire–had connected us. I sat on the monorail a minute longer than the rest as they departed, thinking about what had just occurred: Grandma wanted me to know she had heard me years before worrying about her things. Wow!

Trouble set in at the store where I worked. It was a 7-Eleven type store and the night shift was eerie at times. Thank God I worked with another girl, but still we weren't happy about those customers who came in late, half drunk, looking for trouble, beer, and girls to chase.

One night after getting off work, my car wouldn't start. It was always giving me fits but after I got the hood up to see if anything looked obvious, I saw him coming: a man in a hooded sweatshirt. He grabbed me and tore off my shirt as we struggled.

After a while I got so exhausted, I just pretended to pass out. He saw his opportunity to run, but instead pulled out a pocketknife and cut my throat. It was awful. He waited first to watch me die, and then took off.

Oh God, please help me, I prayed, but knew it was my time. There was no way I was going to survive this at five in the morning without help nearby. (Parking in the store's lot was prohibited, so I was over a block away on an empty road.)

After lifting from my body and looking down on the grisly scene, I said one last prayer–for my parents. I asked God to watch over and protect them from this madman. *If they catch him,* I thought, *they would have to face him at the trial. If they didn't, he might find out where they live.*

So while it is true this man stole my life, it's also true another life came for me. Only this life came as a super bright white light streaming from in front of me. It communicated to me personally, showing me there is a lot more life for me live, and to come right in!

I was gently pulled inside The Light, where I saw me, as a child, jumping rope. Next, images came forward of me bringing pansies to our neighbor, thanking her for the yummy pie she made for us earlier that day. After that I saw continuing images of me doing things that were joyful and loving. Believe me, it's the most tender feeling you can ever imagine to see yourself as a child and feel the true goodness inside you.

After the ladder of time brought me up to present time, I saw me writing down on a piece of paper how much I wanted to be with Grandma and Grandpa again someday. How funny it was to see this because I had written it down not long before.

Just then, after my memory confirmed this image, I saw my grandparents arm-in-arm walking toward me. They looked so young! They still looked like themselves, but nothing like the depleting versions I had witnessed as they wasted away.

"I love you!" I remember yelling at them. They smiled so wide I started running. They explained to me they were beside me when I came home after the funeral for Grandma and hadn't left my side since.

They are my angels, I remember thinking. *God had given them my note!* There it was in Grandma's pocketbook right next to her favorite photos of us and her beloved cat, Angel. Tripping over myself with excitement about seeing them again, I finally asked where we were.

Grandpa sort of stammered out the answer. "We're in Heaven, Erica! Don't you know that? Grandma and I came here when we died, but came back for you whenever you needed us. It's been our turn to be angels, and someday it'll be your turn for someone you love."

Oh my, I thought. *That sounds like a huge responsibility. Who am I to guide someone in life? I was only a clerk in a convenience store who got stabbed for not keeping her eyes open.*

"Boy!" Grandpa said, "Have you got some work to do! You're not *only* anything. You're the best! Somehow you started to believe in the sad things in life instead of the best things, so the sad things convinced you it was your fault you died. Let me talk with you someday about how to reverse your mixed-up thinking," he added.

"I will," I sheepishly said, knowing what he said was true. Why did I buy into the belief my life wasn't worth much? Who told me that, and why didn't I resist them?

After that I recall watching the review of my life which included people behaving as if I was just average, or worse, not worth their time at all. I saw me feeling invisible, as if I didn't matter at all. I even saw how my parents couldn't be bothered to help me anymore because I wasn't their cute little girl.

Stopping to catch my breath I saw my uncle on my dad's side appear. He had died of an aneurism when I was in my early teens. Just like that, he was dead. After dying, he told me, he saw himself the way I was seeing myself, and advised me not to feel bad about anything. "Just learn your lesson that no matter what, you are someone very, very special," he said earnestly. "It's up to you to uncover that. No one else's job. Just yours."

Over the months ahead I figured out he was right. Along with my grandparents, my uncle told me I had been given the gift of musical talent, and as a child I was supposed to have entered into a program of theatre or dance. They said it was advised I begin a program of music right away, so I could catch up with the *real* version of me; the version that is confident and expressive, without fear or doubt about who I am and how truly wonderful I am.

Scared if I could do it (get up in front of others), I gave it the old college try and soon found out it was my passion. I wasn't just good at acting, I found out I was really talented, if I say so, myself. Hundreds of people now come to my performances. All the time. In fact, I've started writing a play I think will be pretty good when all is said and done. In my play, I am the heroine, the one who does amazing things, surprising those who had taken her for granted, thinking she was ordinary.

I love me now! Once it had been my belief if I ever could get to this stage in life I would be in my seventies or eighties, but here I am with my whole life ahead. Luckily, I didn't have to wait that long.

Life is good for you too, whoever you are reading this. I need you to know if you think life is hard, or worse, change the way you think about it because that will reverse the tide. Start telling yourself your money situation is not just going to be good, it's going to be great. Tell yourself you're not just going to date someone you like, you're going to meet and marry the love of your life.

It's important you have these talks with yourself. Otherwise, you'll spend the rest of your days examining your life through other people's ideas of who you are. And that's always wrong, and always a pity.

You're the best! Never forget it. Now go out and live your best life yet!

RAYMOND

Sometimes when you know you're going to die it's a relief. I don't mean it's good to want to die, just that it's good to let go of what's ailing you. When I was dying I knew it because I was a physician in my younger years, but as I got older I also got feeble-minded which, of course, was hard on my family as well as me.

It's always been easy for me to learn and even to keep track of the tiniest of details which is why turning eighty-five was, how shall I say, an enormous milestone. It was an age I thought I might not live to see, so when I arrived there I was amazed but somehow also a little disappointed.

Not today, I told myself inside. *Not today*. Not on my birthday if I can help it. So I put my foot down and stood up one last time and thanked my family and guests for allowing me to be their honored guest. It had been wonderful.

Before I climbed into bed I had a chilliness colder than all the other times in which I knew my body temp had dropped. This time though, it went to my very core. *So, it's going to be tonight,* I guessed. Dropping into a deep sleep I wrestled with my demons. I had visions of old times where I had been unkind to kids my age, and even other adults whom I thought at the time brought it on by their own behavior.

Stubborn, I was. Sullen too, sometimes. Wild thoughts kept pestering me as I slept but the most beautiful thing then started to take place: I dreamed I was on a desert island with sand and water and only a cape to keep the sun off me. *Strange,* I thought, *to have a cape around me but glad for its protection from the overhead sun.* After a while though, the sun dried me out so much the cape no longer offered any protection. In my dream I just laid down on the sand, where it was wet and cool, and tried to survive like that.

Immediately, the sand and water began to cool my temperature and I started feeling better. Opening my eyes as I lay on my back, I saw in the sky a purple rainbow. It was magnificent and yet so unusual. Welling up, tears started rolling down my face. I had seen the bridge to the source of God's innate ability for us to be healed! I knew it when I saw it because I felt it inside. I sensed the miraculous properties in the violet light would lead me into my health again. It would restore my soul, and thereby restore me.

As the dream phased into a faster pace, I felt my mind getting better. Soon I was seeing and thinking again so clearly it was as sharp as when I was a teenager, I swear!

Best I get to the point of this lesson, though. As I lay in my stupor dreaming of the wonderful purple bridge to my restored health, I realized I was decreasing from the world you are still in, and increasing into the world I am now in.

It was a remarkable passageway to come through, I must say. I never thought dying would be like floating over an ocean of fear. That's what our minds are like as we get older and older, at least for most of us. An ocean of fear more and more turbulent due to reasons that never really existed. Just fear they *could* exist.

But soon I was lifting from my body on the bed. I knew then this was no longer a dream because I was no longer on the desert island. After I lodged myself in my room apart from my body, I was unsure where to go or what to do next. I was still myself, just not in myself.

How peculiar it felt to be without my muscular-skeletal body, the one I was so accustomed to and related to throughout my career. Instead of feeling cold or hot, I felt no temperature at all. Relaxing a bit more as I stood there, I grounded myself in the knowing I *could* survive my body and perhaps even have a life that still mattered.

After what seemed like an hour or two of contemplation, I wore out the idea of staying with my body, so began to investigate the house further. Next to my room was my sister's room. She was down with a cold after the party. It came on suddenly so she took to her bed straight away that night.

Left of her room was the outer room where I saw the TV was still on. My sister's teenage grandson was still up, but mostly asleep as he lay watching something about the western cowboy times. Unsure if he could see me, I stood there until he nodded, but then closed his eyes again.

Relaxed. I realized that's why he saw me. He was completely relaxed. It was not so unlikely to him I might be standing there, so he didn't react. After that I made my way into my sister's room in hopes she might be partially awake. She was, but because of the medicine she had taken earlier, her mind was a blur.

Oh well, I thought. *Perhaps it's better I not try to give her too much to think about all in one night: her brother dying, and coming back to see her all inside three hours! What should I do next?* It wasn't time for the family to get up but staying there seemed awkward. So I mentally bid them goodbye and decided to head out the door.

As you probably know, most small towns don't have much going on that time of the night and my town was no exception. Incredible sounds were alive though, and I was intrigued by how much I could hear, really hear.

Pretty soon a dog in the distance barked a couple of times and then came the rabbit jumping through a hole in the fence. I heard it! I distinctly heard a rabbit squeezing through a fence hole, trapped there earlier by the dog chasing it. But this time the dog made the mistake of taking off in the wrong direction when it heard a horn honk, thus allowing the rabbit an escape.

It's still a wonder to me how I knew all this, but I did. Then I just got down off the front porch and started down the driveway when I thought I heard my name. *Raymond.* Inside my head I heard it again. *Raymond.* Without a doubt, my name was being called.

Looking around I had my suspicions my sister must be up, but the lights in the house were still off so that made no sense.

Then I heard it again. *Raymond.* Sister or not, I have to find out who it is. Turning around trying to see in the dimly lit driveway, I saw a woman there but she wasn't like us. She was invisible, mostly. It startled me at first but as I approached her likeness I saw it was my friend, Suzanne.

This isn't making sense, I thought. *She died years ago of pneumonia after I treated her but couldn't get her to turn the corner. How is it she is here?* At that, inside me I heard her explain she was there to take me home. "What?" I uttered. "Take me home? I'm already home, here at my sister's house. This is where I live now."

That's when she laughed and said, "No, not that home. Your real home."

I stood there working this through my mind. Nothing like this had ever happened in my life so I wasn't sure what to say or do. *I think I'm mentally competent,* I remember hoping. *Oh God, what if I'm not?*

Suzanne woke me up some more. "Raymond. Don't be silly. You're fine now. It's just your time to come home. I hope you're ready. It's time. Let's go!"

After that I remember wondering if I was ready. There wasn't much else I could do given I was out of my body, and it was the middle of the night. So I told her we could go, but without much enthusiasm. Shaken, I walked toward her. She was even brighter up close than when I saw her from the top of the driveway. Illuminated by a sort of beam of light, I saw she had come from above.

"It's beautiful there," she assured me. "You won't be back so if you need to say goodbye to anyone, now is the time."

I knew it was time to go but thought it was sweet she was giving me one last chance to say goodbye to my family before I leave my body behind. She knew as a physician I hadn't prepared myself for the inevitable parting of the Red Sea. I did not believe one survived the death of the body, yet here I was sheepishly taking her hand.

Elevating the both of us she lifted us from this prism of light we call Earth. "My job," she described, "is to relax you and get you to understand it's just a matter of letting go and then it happens."

"What happens?" I needed to know.

"Your troubles let go and you just float above them," she reassured me.

Stupid me, I thought. The more I took on in life that seemed important, the more I thought I had a handle on what life was really about. It couldn't have been more the reverse. The ocean of fears I described was the energy around me carrying the weight of all my concerns and contemplations. I had never thought to let those go.

Suzanne held my hand, and we soared up, up, up into what seemed like a ramp or escalator into the wonderful light from above. "Karma," she said. "This is the karma ramp. You get to go pretty high my friend. You had so much positive to say, you are being offered one of the best lives on the other side a man could hope for."

Really? I thought I had been rather sour at times, yet here she was telling me how positive I had been. That made me feel really good so I accepted her offer and went into The Light with her. Soon we were beyond my sister's driveway and then out of the Earth's atmosphere, as far as I could tell.

"What's next?" I asked.

"Well," she said smiling at me, "I get to take you to a reunion with many of those people whose lives you have touched."

What? I thought. "What do you mean?"

Her eyes sparkled which let me know it was okay. So with that we went into a sort of tunnel that was at first rather eerie. It was dark but beyond it a sort of physical light extended itself to us. It was just a small light at first, but it grew larger and larger as it reached us and then guided us through the tunnel. It was unusually quiet but in a matter of minutes, maybe less, we were streaking through it with amazing sights and sounds.

"Love!" she said to me. "You're in the presence of love!" It was overwhelming. The stream taking us forward was suggesting to me I not ever feel shame again; I not ever feel fear again; I not ever feel embarrassment again; I not ever doubt my goodness again. Lovingly it suggested I stay alive and be me, without any excuse for changing who I am.

I was humbled beyond what I can even begin to express if we had eons to converse. But here, in this written form, I just need to emphasize if you do not believe in the afterlife, please reconsider. It's alive, the world I'm in! It's as real as your world, only mine is without the crying and the sorrow. The grief, I think, is what's killing most of us on Earth.

As a physician, I want to take each of you into my heart and assure you are never apart from those you love. If they die, their spirit comes home into The Light where they are restructured back into who they truly are without their doubts and fears. Then they are asked to come back and walk with those they love, assisting them in their decisions to become better and happier people.

How we die is we leak away our life force. I know because as I was losing my muscle strength to stand very long and do anything independently, I walked with much less emphasis. Which, it turns out, took out of my body its force of life. Little do we know our feet draw up from Earth a force of life sustaining us all the days of our lives, if we want it. Of course, when it's your time to come home, you do, but you do *not* have to lose your mind or body in the process of aging.

I get to come back now to those on your side who are open to healing. I know who they are because I can hear and feel them as they come through to my side asking for help. It's been great to get to offer my hand. I hope this message will make its way into your heart so you can offer your hand to someone someday who might need it, too.

While I live here, I long to live again where you are someday. I want to be of service and be back in my God-given body. When Jesus stood in The Light and told me I was an icon of goodness, I cried for what seemed like months. His heart is beyond what we could ever imagine another person's heart could be given all he endured.

But in his light of love, I know he forgave me for those things I felt ashamed about, and I want to offer you this: Offer

Jesus your shame and your sorrows. He is the one human being who walked the Earth and knows how horrible it is to wear those sorrows.

To me he is God, in everyway. I know I don't deserve to be here on your side again giving advice (given how I took God and especially Jesus for granted), but hope it's all the more reason you heed my words to hold tight to the gifts Jesus offers each of us: peace, love, forgiveness and everlasting life.

I'll come around again someday if you need me. Just think about my name and my story. It'll cue me you need me for some reason, any reason, even if it's to talk about the wonders of the universe, or the wonders of a baby as it draws in its first breath of the great, *I AM!*

PEPU and TIAN

I loved life more than maybe anyone else I knew. I wasn't ill or old when I died, I just had a heart attack after moving something heavy. It was awful, I remember that, but at least it was fast.

My name is Pepu. I was a great lover of the outdoors and wished to be there all the time. My career as a puppet maker didn't allow me as much time as I wanted to be outdoors, but it did give me the chance to live free by working for myself and setting my own schedule.

After making human puppets for children, I decided to put my skills into making animals. They were quite popular with crowds when I showed them off at fairs and markets, but it was the dragons that brought me fame where I lived.

Long necks, green scales and bright opulent colors decorated each dragon with hinges on their jaws, necks and appendages which promoted a liquid-like movement. Children and adults alike were mesmerized as the dragons moved with a life-like motion beyond the ordinary.

When I was on your side of the curtain, I took for granted I would live a long and prosperous life. I knew I was on the road to success as my puppets gained popularity and reputation, but success I now know does not ensure a long life.

The dragons I crafted were not happy-looking dragons, of course. Made to ward off evil spirits, they had to have fierce faces. It was a marvel of creativity, I felt, to make these faces come alive! They brought much happiness and gaiety to my patrons as they acquired them for their homes and workplaces.

Training to do this work came through my grandparents. My grandfather brought with him from China all the traditions of the old country, including woodworking and painting skills. Incredibly, my grandmother taught me the written language through ancient Chinese children's tales, which later gained me access into Chinese circles of influence I would not have realized otherwise.

By making these traditional dragon puppets, some larger than others, I became a man of wealth. It was a surprise to me how fast it happened. As the orders poured in, my spending habits remained the same, so my nest egg grew.

Eventually I drew tired of making dragons, and Spirit moved me to open a store of my own where I put the most beautiful of all my dragons in the window, along with other Chinese treasures. By far, however, the dragon is what drew people in along with their pocketbooks.

After one shop, the second opened and soon the third. Before long I had many shops and in each window hung one of my giant creations protecting the health and wealth of those who sought the dragon's powers and influence.

Because the puppets were taken to be such creations of art and not just omens of good fortune, I was pressed more and more to open a factory; to build them through laborers. Today there are many stores and restaurants with my beautiful dragons in their entryways, guarding and protecting them while adding the artistic style of ancient China for all to see and appreciate.

My days were long with necessary duties, but the evenings still gave me time to walk and think. Suddenly, however, one day as I was moving a giant crate to the other side of the room I was seized with pain, excruciating pain, and doubled up on the floor where I was not discovered for hours.

My day had come. I had died. My sister, Tian, who had died as an infant, was the first to greet me in The Light. I knew her instantly because she had my mother's face and my father's smile. She held out her hands to me, to help release me from my body. She was like an angel. Beautiful, like silk, she shown in The Light.

When I took her hand, she showed me my body below as we rose up, and suggested I bid it farewell, to bless it one last time. Upon doing so, I felt a final release from my body. I was free!

I went willingly with Tian because in her beauty and presence I could sense we had been together throughout our lives and she knew what was best. I became her little brother and fought nothing she suggested.

Eventually, we entered what seemed like a place of worship. It was a large hall with many people praying to God asking for mercy. It was grand hall. I sensed millions of prayers had been sung there. Its atmosphere felt warm and inspiring. Tian told me it was her favorite place to come after she walked through the veil to see us, so she could then pray for what we needed.

I was profoundly moved by what she taught me. She said she was able to travel to be with us whenever we needed her. She showed me the iron in her body was not normal as a baby, so she died. But she also showed me the gift of being without iron meant she could travel between the planes without difficulty.

Traveling between the planes meant she just had to think of us with our heavier, mortal bodies, and eventually she could see us, one by one. "It's like that," she told me. "Once you learn to ask for what you want, it comes to you. But you have to be quiet and simply wait. In time it appears."

Many who cross over are under the belief they can no longer cross back to see their families. They are so used to the idea our worlds are separate, they have to be taught to see your side again with their eyes attuned to metal iron.

Now, for the reason I am here: Tian and I want you to learn to squeeze your eyes shut very tightly. So tightly it might almost become uncomfortable. After you do, slowly open your eyes and learn to see "the light people" with your corrected vision.

It takes practice and belief, but we know you can do it. Place our names together at the top of our story please. We travel everywhere together these days in hopes of being able to help those who want to help mankind raise the veil between our two worlds.

Be kind to your husbands and wives, and your children will bless you with grandchildren that curse the Earth no more.

NICK

I was minding my own business when I saw what I thought was a building on fire. It was a house with smoke pouring out of its windows everywhere. Before I could call 911, I heard a scream for help.

Putting down my groceries, I ran into it but quickly lost my way in the thick dark smoke. Again I heard the sound of someone calling for help–a child maybe, it sounded so weak–so I tried to keep going.

I kicked in a door that was partially open and noticed an old man on the floor with nothing over him, like a wet rag to protect him. It was awful, the look on his face as I rolled him over. He was wearing a frozen look of panic.

Next I went into the adjoining room where I found his wife. She was the one I had heard. I recognized her trembling voice, so at least I started to feel better that I had caught up with the person pleading for help.

Her hands were dark already from a lack of oxygen. I knew we had only seconds to get fresh air or we'd both perish, but her primary concern was for her husband so I told her he got out okay.

Next to her was her Pekinese or Maltese dog, already choking on its vomit. Her nose was so badly injured by this time she hadn't noticed its demise. I scooped her up and went to go out another door through the back, but it was already jammed shut from the fire damage.

I asked if there was another route outside not through the front room (since I didn't want to frighten her by seeing her dead husband), but she said no, only through the windows maybe.

At that I kicked out a kitchen window. It was awful. The smoke came rushing toward us like a monster. We choked and coughed so badly it alone nearly killed us.

As I ran around looking for a cloth to cover our mouths, I realized I had lost her in the kitchen. Calling out, I got no response. By then she had surely submitted to the smoke and died. *Oh God*, I thought, *what have I done? What if I had just called 911?*

At that moment a smoky white light entered the room exactly where I was standing. It was a beautiful white being! An angel, I think. It smiled calmly at me and asked if I was ready to come into The Light and be saved.

I went, but was unsure who or what this magnificent being was. All I knew was it seemed to have the know-how to get us out alive. I could feel as I took this being's hand, I too felt like smoky white light. I could actually feel the essence of myself evaporating into a sort of stream, whereby I could immerse myself into its matter.

"Lost but found," was all I could think about and feel. Beautiful white smoky light. I'm a part of this real yet unreal feeling. How wonderful and mysterious! Life is beyond what we think it is!

At that point I lost consciousness yet remember the feeling of floating. Like being on your back in a boat, asleep. You can feel the boat's movement to and fro, without anything rushing or bumping it. Just calm and easy.

Little by little I awoke to the feeling I was being tended to. It was awful for a minute remembering the flames and smoke, but then I saw the rest of where I was, which was in a new room. It was yellow, mostly. Sunny yellow.

Outside I could hear chirping. Birds singing and squawking near my window as if to let me know they were there. I loved it. I loved waking up that way!

Next, I drew my attention to the fact I was in a lounge chair, like those on ships. It was comfortable and I was relaxed, but how did I get there?

Just as I was thinking about this a nurse walked in. Her mouth wasn't moving but I could hear her inside telling me not to worry. She said on the other side I was in a house fire and saved an old woman's life. She said the woman passed out, but the broken window provided an evacuation point for the firemen to see so they got to her in time.

As she told me this I knew my body hadn't made it. Although I thought about calling 911, the better part of me wanted to be of assistance. Now I think that same better part of me also knew I wasn't going to make it out alive.

I still think about it on occasion. What if I hadn't gone in? What if the fire department had made it there first? Would I still be alive on your side? Would this be my wish if I had the choice?

It's a funny thing when you're on my side. Your mind is active and your heart still beats but your body is just made of light. Life is easier, that's for sure, but you do think about the times when your body made you feel alive and vibrant, too. At least I do.

Whenever I come to that place, I get to come back and be an unseen guide to someone who regrets life. I get to place my hand on their shoulder and utter into their mind that life is wonderful if they just let it be.

That said, I want to walk with you now and explain further why those of us on my side shouldn't come back too soon. Though you go through a review when you die, you also see why you made the decisions you made.

In that review you feel all those feelings again, which is very turbulent and overwhelming for many people. For me, it was awful and wonderful. I felt my heart breaking over love again, and my mind wanting to go everywhere and explore everything. Life is a gift, but you have to endure the hard stuff to realize the gift is still there *if* you want it.

For many, they are so damaged by life they do not want to come back, even to be of inspirational help to others. They only want to be apart from the circumstances that took them to their fate.

I wanted to come back and be a guide. I love my family. My sister who is mentally retarded is the one truly good human being I know. Not a sinister bone in her body. Her world is almost like mine now. She knows not to necessarily believe in all what we "normal" people claim is truth. Although she wanders around in her own world, she is protected and shielded from sad thoughts for the most part.

Of course, when I died she went around looking for me. After a while I think she knew deep down I wasn't coming back, but she never regretted that I went into the fire to help strangers. To her I was a hero, so that's how I should be remembered by everyone.

Life is about growing up inside, I now know. I never understood that when I was on your side. I guess I just assumed you grew up inside just like you do outside. But the fact is, nearly everyone is repressed in some manner which keeps them from living their fullest life.

Looking at my life has been extremely important. While it serves me to know myself better, it truly serves others, too. I now get it why men make the mistake of being self-centered when they should be more empathetic. I get it they just can't open themselves up to the feelings they have inside that they are just as vulnerable to death as everyone else.

Sound familiar? Men are running away from death almost all of their lives. It's true! Even those who run into burning buildings or jump from ledges pulling parachute cords at the last second. They spend their time trying to cheat death. It's always been that way. Death is on their minds and they want to win!

I am (excuse my humor) living proof this is what men do. I loved life with all my heart. I never wanted it to end. I wanted nothing in my way like an illness or accident to keep me from having everything in life at my fingertips.

Stopping to think about this was my assignment from elders. Many wonderful men who know about these things have counseled me about my nature, and how it could be championed into leadership for causes like world peace and activism for environmental causes.

Who would believe that's why God gave us this hunger for life? It is about having fun in all you do, not about cheating death by climbing the highest cliffs. It's about taking a hold of life's greatest challenges facing mankind and then doing something about it.

Starvation. War. Disease. Global warming. Need I go on? What's in your community needing your leadership?

If I could come back, I would tell every man, woman and child to find a cause that matters to them and then pour their hearts into it. Their life will come together when they do. It's like that you know. When you give to others something that matters, you get back a life that matters.

My name is Nick. My cause now is helping others to learn to give of their hearts and time. Because, no matter how much you give, if you do it for a cause important to mankind, you'll always want to give more. Can you imagine spending the rest of your life tending to the needs of others instead of your own? Who's the hero then?

Not too long from now I'll come back into my own life. It's called the Second Coming. It means I'll run up to my sister, hug her, and neither of us will remember I was away. It means I'll be a better human being in general, which will have an enormous impact on the planet, and we'll all be the better for it.

I love you all. Thank you from the bottom of my heart for caring enough to read my story.

ELIZABETH

For those who have died and crossed over, the afterlife is amazing. It's incredible in that when you die you receive your *real* body. Where you are now, you wear your mask. But when you die, you release it and go into your real self, which reveals your real mind and body.

Coming into The Light itself is easy when you release from your body without regret. But for those who have not let go of their life, the journey itself can be a challenge. That's where I come in. I help people to prepare for what's ahead, which is spectacular.

Starting with the day I died, I wasn't ill or concerned about much that morning. In fact, I was just thinking it was an ordinary kind of day as I was getting things ready for my hop on the train. I loved the train because I could get a little shuteye or read, each of which put me in a calm mood before I came into work as an orthodontist.

As my city life gained speed, meaning my client work and friendships really took off, I had much to think about so rarely spent time working on myself; on being more self aware. As you get older and older, you just sort of accept you are who you are, and the world is what it is, but that's not true or real when you step back and see through the eyes of love why things are as they are.

Anyway, as I was waiting for my train I leaned forward for a second to see if I could spot it and that's when it happened. I fell from the platform onto the tracks below. I started to get up but it was too late. The train had arrived on time.

Once it happened it was done. There was no more realization of my body as I knew it. From that moment on I walked without my legs and saw without my eyes. It's supernatural, I know, but it's the suddenness of my accident that got me right into my light body.

Bright lights then started to appear from everywhere. It was as if the sky was aglow with sparkles, only these were drawing closer and closer toward me. I think I was still amazed and in awe of my lightness because what I did next was funny: I stood there looking up.

There in the sky I saw a cloud hovering over me, swirling around like you see when helicopters kick up loose dirt below. It was wide but not very wide. Just wide enough I could see the sides, top, and bottom which was now just landing at my feet.

Reeling with excitement, I saw through that swirling cloud–that funnel of love–The Lord coming for me. It was a vision and a voyage I'll never forget.

As I rose from the ground, I looked back to see my old self on the tracks, but never would I look back again after that. Before my eyes I saw the spectacle of love described as The Light, only it also had a face and awaiting arms. It was Jesus Christ, himself.

I declare, I thought I *must* have died and gone right into Heaven because there he was. But instead of taking me further in, Jesus said I had an accident and could not yet come all the way through the tunnel because my time wasn't yet complete. He explained my soul was still immature and needed more lessons so I could someday feel I drove myself into The Light without an accidental death.

Alone now in The Lord's tunnel, I felt the grip of disappointment as I heard the words that I was not yet ready to come home and be with Jesus. His was the one hand on Earth I could feel contains everything we need in order to become a race of loving, forgiving, and peaceful human beings. He is the one, I know, who then guided me back into my body to show me the rest of my life.

Strong currents of electricity then raced through my body. Without knowing how, I was suddenly back in it, bruised and battered but alive. Those at the station were now all around me as I heard them saying over and over, "Don't move. We're getting help. You'll be all right."

Then more strong currents came over me only this time it was as if I had recovery paddles on my chest. This was from The Lord. I saw the ray of light from above coming down, penetrating my forehead, which was when the Garden of Eden started unfolding for me to see.

As a child I recall the story being told to me about the Garden of Eden. It sounded like an exotic place full of foliage and fruits. But never did anyone describe for me the way the light itself is extreme and smiles at you. It does! You can feel it all around you with the same passion you felt when your parents smiled at you when you were little. As it embraces you, never do you feel rejected or empty in any measure.

Little by little I was extracted from my body on the tracks. Speckles of light came into the space where my cells had been just moments before. It was a song, playing as my new body began relating to itself as pure love.

Commencing from there, I gave into the experience because the rest happened with such speed to describe it would be impossible.

Humble. I was humble and trembling. Because my experience in this place so bright with light was new, I felt myself being calmed by the presence of Olivia, my mother's old housekeeper from my childhood. We were close then. I regarded her more as a mother than my own. Together we stood beaming into one another's eyes, and then I broke into laughter with the delight that at long last we were reunited.

Olivia's warmth was exactly as it once was. It was as if we hadn't been apart at all; as if she still saw me as that funny freckled child she knew and loved so long ago. I felt it inside! I felt her feeling how our love was still as precious and alive as ever.

At that point my chest became so warm I felt sure I could fly with exaltation. Love is like that, you know. It's alive like a magical flower that grows larger and larger when you ask it a question from your heart, or shrinks when you retreat from it.

This was not something I had ever thought about before, but I want you to know your heart contains the seeds of atomic power; of atomic energy. And when you decide you need to be restored via the power of prayer, you will be allowed to give the world the known answer to all of its problems: *LOVE*.

Cleaning up the rivers is important. Keeping watch over our children from predators is important. Behaving kindly to strangers is important. But none of it matters the way your life of hope and love does.

Believe in your heart's ability to drive you toward more and more love when you say you desire more and more love. Believe in peacemakers from all across the globe softly coming into your reality when you ask for peace from every corner of the world. If you do, I promise you will never hear what I had to hear: you're not yet ready to come all the way home.

As a child I wrote my brother Tag a letter telling him how much I missed him and hoped he would come back soon. I saw my mother's eyes filling with tears because she knew he wouldn't be coming back since he had just died in Viet Nam. I saw her world crumbling around her.

But now in The Light, amazingly I saw Tag standing there with my note in his hand. Excitedly, he held out his arms and we hugged for what seemed like the better part of my life.

It's like that. The further and further you go into The Light the more and more deeply you see and feel things, where things just seem to fit together and make sense more and more.

I wanted to come to you, each of you, through Lynn's help today, to let you know if you have ever written anything down on paper and asked The Lord to send it to your loved one on the other side, it does appear to them.

Things of value to the heart never cease. They come with you. Can you imagine? Nothing ordinary exists where I am. Just those things you treasure!

After seeing Tag and Olivia, I traveled even further into The Light where I saw my daily life. It was like an exhibit, a three-dimensional overview of all I had thought and felt. While that alone should be amazing enough, it wasn't until I came to the realization that every decision I made is what charted my life, did I come *all the way* into The Light.

Once I saw I was not a victim of anyone other than my own fears, I started to relate to myself as someone who had many more choices and outcomes than I ever realized. It was then The Lord (who had never fully backed away from me) took me into the corridor of my future and showed me the special gifts I have as a communicator of human love.

There, The Lord showed me that all the while I sang and told stories of love as a child, I was promised someday I would be able to come into a life where I could hear and communicate through the veil of disbelief. The Lord showed me that while my accident was untimely, it didn't mean my life's calling to be a communicator of love had to end.

Since then, I have accepted many callings to communicate with people on your side working hard to hear from people they love over here. Hundreds of parents, spouses, and children ache from the tremendous loss of their loved ones, and need my help.

It's my work and pleasure to help them hear my words ministering to their hearts. Someday, maybe I can be of help to you if you ask for messages from your loved ones. Be patient, though. Sometimes it takes a while for each of us to feel one another's vibrations and attune to them.

Terrible tragedies happen every day. But if you believe in Jesus Christ, your soul is washed clean and you go traveling with The Light. There, you go with your loved ones and feel what it is like to make lives even better on both sides.

Jesus came for me once and will come back for me soon. I know this because I feel it in my heart. In the meantime, I get to do things for many people like Lynn Scott by staying close to them, giving inspiration and ideas that help crease into their hearts that *miracles are possible.*

Strong winds are blowing. Be certain your world is one with Jesus, for he is accompanying a band of angels, like me, to come for YOU!

JESSE

The light that day was overcast. Everything was silver, I remember. The water had frozen in our house so I had gone outside to play when I met up with my pals and decided to go ice skating. While our neighbor's farm was small compared to ours, they had a pond. In the summer we used it a lot for keeping cool, but this was the first time it seemed cold enough for skating.

After horsing around for a while trying to poke holes through the ice with sticks, we started to race. While I was fast, my friend Ricky was lightening fast. Apart we were brothers of the same soul. Together we were adversaries in our competitive drives.

As the sun came up a little higher, I remember noticing the water underneath shining up through the ice. Before I could think about it twice, it cracked and I quickly slid under. Almost immediately I knew I was ill-fated. With all their might my friends tried and tried to pull me out, but even Ricky, the tallest and strongest, didn't have a long enough reach after throwing his jacket to me to hang onto. Besides, I was too tired. The draining feeling had begun.

For those of you who haven't almost died, you're probably not familiar with the draining feeling. It's a particular sensation specific to dying: the feeling that your very life force is leaking out. For me it was the feeling of being pulled down. Not by my weight, but by my depleting energy. It felt like the smallest bits barely left of me were on an escalator going down.

Softly I remember thinking, *This is it. I am going to die and I'm only in the sixth grade.* While I hadn't put much consideration into death before (other than when my grandma died after a long illness), it was without a doubt my turn now.

Bad grades were always a problem for me. While I was smart, I was not really interested in school, always preferring to be outside. For some crazy reason though, as I slowly immersed, my grades kept crossing my mind. *Why do I keep thinking about my grades?* I remember wondering. Then everything went silent for what seemed like a deep period of time.

"Jesse...Jesse..." Silence, and then again it came, "Jesse...are you ready?" Who was that? Whoever it was I heard them as clearly as if they were right next to me.

"Ready for what?" I sleepily thought back.

"Are you ready for the rest of your life?" the voice asked.

This gave me pause. *Am I ready for the rest of my life?* It seemed strange to ask a drowning person if they are ready to be saved.

"Yes! I'm ready," I thought back with a bit more energy. "But I need help. I can't move my body. Help me..."

While the water's surface above me moved purposefully with shimmering movements, it now had a particular sort of energy ring surrounding the lip of ice where I had come through, glowing as if it were on fire from within.

"Help me..." I thought again while focusing on this ring of light. Then, suddenly and with incredible clarity, I saw the spirit of Jesus Christ coming to me through that ring. He, himself, pulled me from that watery grave. Together we soared up and out of that pond, above the clouds, high into the universe where all must come when it's their time.

"Jesus, you came for me," I said to him deep from within my heart.

"I've always been with you, Jesse. It's just that today is the day you get to *see* me as we come home together."

"I hope you know me," I cried inside. "I'm not good at many things. If you are upset with me and took me away from my home because I'm not good in school, please let me go back so I can try harder. I promise I will."

"Home, Jesse, is here with me. All the while you have been with your parents, you have also been with me. I've watched you everyday of your life and know every thought and feeling you've had. To me you are perfect. I know you think you are not, but you are. Can you believe me, Jesse?"

This was unbelievable! I was perfect? I knew Jesus was God (according to my grandma), but it sure didn't seem like he really knew me. *Wait until he finds out who I really am,* I secretly thought. *He'll have to change his mind then.*

"I have your heart in my heart, Jesse. Did you know that? I feel the very core of who you are. No matter what you do, I know who you really are, and you are perfect."

Somehow this time I felt his words of absolute unconditional love as they poured over me, coating me from head to toe. It was then, for the first time in my life, I recall feeling I had nothing to fear. I was with Jesus, himself, and he wanted me to know I am a part of him.

Coming higher and higher into The Light with Jesus was the most remarkable and spectacular thing imaginable. Above us a passageway opened up in the sky like a secret gate and through it we passed into an exact duplicate world of Earth. It was beautiful and shiny just like the pictures NASA sends back from outer space, only this Earth, Jesus told me, is different. I felt special hearing this, and curious, too.

"This Earth," Jesus said, "is reserved for those who want to make peace, and free themselves from the chains of fear that bind them."

This is where you get to go, I found out, when you decide you're truly ready to reach up to God and declare love *is* the most important thing that exists.

"I don't recall declaring that," I confessed to Jesus. "I've never thought that much about love."

Jesus smiled at me and said, "Many, many times throughout your life, Jesse, you have asked deep from within why people couldn't just enjoy their lives and not hassle one another about stuff that doesn't really matter. Does that sound familiar?"

I smiled back because those were exactly my thoughts, many, many times.

Jesus put his arm around my shoulder and said, "That's when my heart told me you were ready to release from the old Earth, Jesse, and come into the new Earth built through love."

As I thought about the new Earth concept, I remember thinking this had turned out to be a long ride, even though it seemed like only a second or two had passed. As time sped, I saw my old world concentrate into visions of me playing, sleeping and going to school. I saw me asking for things, getting some of them, and doing chores.

After seeing these images, I quietly asked Jesus why I had been so miserable at school. He then showed me the reverse side of the tunnel where in his new Earth I had always been with him and loved school. There, most of my classes were outdoors. As I was playing I was learning—and quickly! I saw me swinging and reciting my multiplication tables out loud at the same time, which meant so much to me because I could never catch onto them before.

Jesus told me there are many kids who never like school because their hearts aren't into it. By going outdoors and putting their classes together with fun, they increase their heart rates and then learning comes easily.

"I love you," I remember telling Jesus as he looked at me softly.

"I love you too, Jesse," he said without a moment's pause. "Jesse, I need you to know I am very proud of you. It's important to me you know that."

"Proud of me for what?" I was almost afraid to ask.

"For being you," he told me. "There were many times you were confronted by others to become someone you weren't. Sometimes it was hard to say no, but you did it. You stayed true to yourself, which meant you stayed true to your nature as my child."

I felt complete at that moment with warmth resurging through me once again, inside and out. I then added something that seemed deeply important to me, "I harmed no one, Jesus."

With that his eyes sparkled and he said, "I am *very* happy you now know how truly wonderful you are, Jesse."

"How far are we going?" I asked.

"We'll be going only as far as your back yard, Jesse," Jesus said, which surprised me because it seemed like that would have been an easy, short journey.

"Then why is this taking so long to get there?" I asked.

Jesus softened his words, "It's not being built very fast, Jesse. Many aren't sure if their home feels like Heaven or not, and have complaints. Until enough decide their home is a wonderful place, it won't be ready for them to come into."

"If it's not ready, then where are we going today?"

Jesus smiled at me. From head to toe I had the feeling we were going somewhere wonderful. "I need you to be with me," Jesus said, "and help build the rest of Earth with homes that feel like Heaven for everyone."

Taking me further and further into The Light, Jesus showed me how the Eiffel Tower is a living beacon of freedom that carries the cross of Jesus, mathematically, in its design because it was issued to its architect that way.

I saw that memories of beauty on Earth are regarded as Jesus' poetry. I saw as Jesus numbers our days here, he needs us to regard his finest works as *miracles of mankind*. He wants us to feel his heart and hands are alive and well within those who create such masterpieces as the Eiffel Tower.

"Come with me," Jesus said as we gently glided above the Paris landscape. "Do you see the way the people talk and interact? Do you sense the passion and pride they feel within their world of beauty? Each is held in high esteem, and place a value in being able to speak their minds as they feel life's gifts through their hearts."

Together, we heard and felt the French Revolution open a gateway to independence. Together, we saw and felt the beating of the hearts of French nationals taking God into their hearts declaring the need to live free or die. Together, we watched this nation build its icon to the world of freedom!

When we carried that love for mankind into our souls, Jesus told me he wished all mankind would accept him as their Savior. We would *all* then be able to soar above the old world where some believe God loves them more than others. They are the ones left behind. But for those who accept Jesus' soul, each is carried into The Light through love.

I was completely stunned! All my questions about God had been answered. I now know when you accept Jesus Christ as your Savior your heart softens. You accept the most important ladder of time there is, which embodies and soars you above those old, dying ways of Earth.

I'm not a boy any longer. I'm an adult man in the visible plane of Earth called water, which is love. I am embodied in light, which makes me shimmer for those whose eyes have adapted to Jesus' Second Coming; however, most have not yet undertaken their eyes of glory.

Because I was invited to be heard by Lynn Scott, I am making my way back to your side without my old body but with my new one. It's a shame I cannot yet make my eyes be seen because they are filled with love for allowing me to tell my wonderful story of love–precious, precious love.

HENRY

Hi. I'm Henry. I've gotten to come through today because in my line of work as a janitor in a school for troubled boys, I've noticed boys are disrespectful to their elders until one or more of the elders stares them down long enough to let them know they're not going to get away with ruining it for all the others.

Studies show when a boy is disrespectful to others, it's because no one challenges them in the eyes. Sometimes, someone will challenge them with their fists, their bodies, or by withholding something they want, but in reality none of that will calm the boy down until he feels for himself that they mean what they say.

It's important to me I have this chance to communicate with you today because I was once just like these boys–ready to give it to anyone who challenged me, and easily upset if I didn't get my own way.

In reality, I didn't want to have everything my way. I was just hoping someone, someday, would come along who wasn't going to tell me I had to do it their way or else. (It's not a genuinely good plan to tell a kid they're already going to lose before they get started. It minces their brains into thinking all things in life are a battle.)

One afternoon before going to work I was just lying on my couch looking up at the ceiling in the living room. I wasn't staring at anything important, just thinking about my grandmother who was important. That's when it happened. I heard inside my head I was going to die in a plane crash in four months. What?

I wasn't going away or on vacation. Who was saying this? And what kind of sick joke was this?

I fell asleep. From there I sort of drifted in and out of consciousness more than sleep it seemed because I remember being led out of town, but not understanding who was leading me, where we were going, or why.

From there I guess I woke up. Due to the time I had to get going. Rushing, I made it to work just in time. Thank goodness traffic was light.

Sanding the floors was on the day's agenda. It's not like buffing the floors anymore, more like sanding them. Because the floors have gotten so beaten up over the years where the boys play, the old buffer now sands them more than polishes.

Anyway, I was working on the floors late in the afternoon when a shot fired. I heard the sound of it over the electric buffer, which, believe me, is loud. I ran outside in the direction of the shot and found the director of the school lying there.

It wasn't my idea to give him mouth-to-mouth. Someone else by that time had shown up and started yelling at me to do it while they ran to get help. So I leaned down but first took a look at him. Ugly. Badly blown apart. His head wound was beyond repair I knew, but for some reason I decided to go ahead and try resuscitating him.

His blood tasted awful in my mouth, but after the initial shock of it I got rid of my fear and tried with all my might to push air into his lungs. They shot up and down which made it look like he was still alive, but knew from the empty look in his eyes he was mostly gone or already dead.

Sad, I thought. *I think he has a family not too far from here. His elderly mom and dad have even come to one or two of the school functions. Pity. Who would tell his family what happened? And what did happen? If someone shot him, are they still around?*

For some reason I grabbed for his hand as I looked down, and there it was, a gun. I couldn't believe my eyes. He had a gun in his hands. Why? What was so awful he couldn't work it out? Why would someone take his own life when so many people loved and relied on him?

I thought about all this in a split second. Amazing how much thought can be crammed into a second or two, but my mind was whirling about this man's life and I couldn't seem to get it to stop.

Life, I thought, as I looked up at the sky. *What is life? Is it about numbers, years, moments, actions, decisions? What is it? Who can tell me?*

When I got back home that evening, I slept harder than ever before. It was as if I had gone into a deeper silence than I ever believed possible. *How weird,* I thought, *to be in the darkest place and still feel okay.* My sleep was solid, not fitful. Strange, after what I had gone through, you'd think I would have had a restless night.

It was now 4:00 a.m., and I was wide awake. Bright eyed and clear-minded, it was as if I had journeyed to a place where none of life's craziness could follow me.

Getting up I noticed the clock on my dresser had stopped at two minutes after midnight. *Hmmm...that's odd.* The electricity hadn't gone out, and I could see it was still plugged in. What would have made it stop? I was curious about it for a minute but then just let it go and started to turn away.

Suddenly, the clock started up again! How weird was *that?* I was looking at it when it seemed to start itself! Or was it a coincidence it restarted just as I was about to walk away?

At that point I instinctively knew it wasn't a coincidence because I wasn't alone. I was a man living alone, but wasn't alone. Someone was there. It sort of creeped me out to think a stranger was there who I couldn't see, but I know I did feel someone's presence.

As all these thoughts were rushing through my mind, my alarm clock rang. Loudly. It went off on its own. No doubt about that, because I hadn't set it. I never had to set a clock. My internal clock was more reliable than any store-bought one.

Without looking around to see who or what I could see, I ran to turn it off. As I passed the mirror, I thought for a second I saw my dad in it. Freak me out! My dad, who died of cancer nine years before, was in the mirror. Whoa.

Okay, I thought. *This is going to be another bizarre day. Just one thing after the other.* So I turned on the TV to get some sound into the room and fell back into a deep, deep sleep.

When I was giving mouth-to-mouth to the dying director, what I didn't know then was my dad was next to me helping me to decide to do it. I learned this from my dream. My dad who had died alone wanted me to be with for this poor fellow to offer him some help. "It really does matter," my dad said to me in my dream.

Stopping the dream I awoke to my alarm clock going off again. This time it said 7:55 a.m. Exactly the right time to get up. How did it self-correct? I hadn't adjusted it. Mostly I just disregarded it by pretending it didn't happen.

As I got out of bed making my way through my daily to-dos, again I heard I had just about four months left before the plane crash. This time though, it came with the added consideration not do anything I would regret. *How could this be? I'm not going on a plane. Why isn't this message going away since I won't be on a plane?*

In less than a month's time I took out an ad to sell my condo. It was just too weird to stay there after all that paranormal stuff. And besides, since the death of the director I wanted to do something more substantial than just clean floors and empty wastebaskets the rest of my life.

When the ad ran, I took advantage of people looking at the place by telling them my neighbors were great and we all got along just fine with parking, etc. The truth was, someone was always pissed off about not getting their particular parking spot, but I needed to get out of there and wasn't about to let something stupid like that make or break a deal.

Soon I had a sale. An elderly couple looking to downsize bought it. It was their dream, they said, to come back to the neighborhood and be near their grandchildren. *Wow,* I thought, *a win-win. Can't beat that!*

Frightened only a little at this point about the plane crash messages, I pressed on and got myself a better place just a little further out of town for even less money. I moved in and felt great!

Great, I thought. *I feel great! I'm here in my dream place without a major mortgage payment, and the old folks get to see their grandkids. Life is good. I'm ready now for the best part of my life.*

Ever since seeing my dad in the mirror, it got me thinking about a lot of things. Not just changing where I lived, but how I lived. Just seeing him for that split second got me wanting more for myself and out of life. It was like an itch I had to scratch.

Life is good, I thought again. And then it happened. A small-engine plane came tearing through the side of the building, right into my new place. I was pinned under it all the while the engine was still making noise. *Is this how my life's going to end?* I thought. *Was I going to die alone? Would someone come for me?* "Help!" I cried. But no one heard me, nor could I hear myself because my voice wasn't there.

Before I die, I thought, *God help me to get rid of my guilt. I did deceive that old couple. I know I shouldn't have lied about the parking. I placed them in a real disadvantage when their family comes to visit. Why was I so selfish? I hope they can forgive me when the time comes to have family over but can't park anywhere nearby because of my crazy neighbors.*

So quiet now. Stillness like the dawn. A deep, deep calmness mercifully came over me. No longer did I fight my feelings about being selfish with the couple who bought my place. *I'll rest for a minute,* I thought, and then it happened: the strings of lights!

Imagine, you're not fully awake or fully asleep, but through the blur you see amazing strings of lights all coming from you. It was as if I was the center of a web and the strings all pulled from me with lights attached to them. *How wonderful!* I thought. *I'm on fire but not with flames, with lights! I'm aglow!* Fully awake then, I was without sleepiness suppressing me at all.

With that, I realized one of the lines of lights was pulling on me a little stronger than the others. They were all attached, onward from somewhere, but only one was particularly strong in its attachment and pull. It was to my dad.

And then I saw him! Beyond the grave there *is* life again! My dad was standing there wearing the shirt I had given him, of mine, which when he was dying said made him feel better. It gave him strength, he insisted.

I'm almost there, Dad, I thought. *I'm coming!* At that I shot forward into the brightest light there has ever been for anyone to see. There, I became engulfed in my own life, only this was my life free of any fears, doubts, or worries.

Home! I'm home! I can feel even the tiniest feelings of the smallest objects I see. An insect walking across a branch made my eyes light up with its antennae, because I knew instinctively the bug used its antennae to reach up and feel The Light.

I came apart at the seams under that airplane's engine, but I've been brought back together here in The Light. I'm a free man, and I've got so much life to live.

My name is Henry, and I'm a darned good janitor who took home with him the wisdom and insight that if men of goodness would only look boys of trouble in the eyes long enough to stare down their fears, the boy's sickness over being unloved and uncared for would release.

I've given you some of my life's story which is enough for now, but I want to close with the help of my dad who wore me out telling me how proud he was of me in my final days for hearing him and even seeing him in the mirror. He knew my time was coming, he said, and wanted me to be prepared. Smiling, he said he was impressed with my inner clock. "It's a hum-dinger!" he added as he laughed.

I love you and thank you all for reading my story. I'm humbled by the response I'm feeling already in my heart by your actions to stop acting as though words don't matter. They do. Tell the truth and let God do the rest!

ANGELA and SUSAN

If you ever had an operation, you know how difficult it is to awaken from the anesthesia. Your mind wanders around for a while trying to make sense of what you are hearing in the background, all the while unsure of why you are where you are.

My story begins in the operating room. I was completely under when my friend, Susan, came to me in my thoughts saying it was my time to come home. I heard her friendly voice and knew who it was, but couldn't make sense of why she was there. She had died over ten years before.

The last time Susan and I saw one another, she was gravely ill in bed, chronically coughing from terminal lung cancer. We were only in our mid-forties, but to be truthful, she looked sixty-five or seventy. After that, she died.

When I felt her touching my hand during the operation, I was overjoyed because it had been a mystery to me where one goes after death. So when she came to let me know it was my time to come home, I considered it for a minute and then spoke back through my thoughts asking if she was going to stay with me if I died.

She smiled (I felt it inside) and said that's why she was there, for exactly that purpose. I relaxed a little and then started to feel a tremendous weight coming off my shoulders; the weight that I had to "do" anything, ever again.

Isn't that an odd thing? I never really realized how much time and effort I was constantly putting into organizing things in my life according to their priority each day. Almost every morning as I thought about my work at the office, I started feeling my energy go there even before I did. After I arrived at work and tried to concentrate on my clients' needs, I began to feel the pressure of my family's needs. Some days it felt as though I would split in half because there would never be enough hours in the day to satisfy all those who counted on me.

But coming back to the day of my departure: I knew it was my time as I felt the lifting of my worries and concerns coming off of me. Though it came as a great relief to go, I knew it meant leaving work behind for others to do.

As Susan warmed my hand in hers, I realized it wasn't the same as when holding someone else's hand. This warmth was more like energy pulses and tingles; like the feeling I got when my hand was numb but then the circulation came back.

As I felt this energy, I realized I was warming up and waking up throughout. It wasn't like waking up in the sense of opening my eyes and seeing what was happening, but I could feel a discernable difference in my way of thinking and observing which had a clarity of its own.

Once I let Susan know I was ready to go with her, she asked me to try to make her face visible in my mind. While that sounded easy because we had many years of fun together, the only images at first that came to mind were of her dying. But as she pressed my hand more confidently, I felt tears of joy return along with the vibrant image of her, healthy and happy.

So there I was on the operating table with my best friend, Susan, at my side. Background sounds of the anesthesiologist asking for more time filtered in. As the surgeon urged him not to be too long, he pushed into my veins something powerful that completely knocked me out–of my body. No more drifting back and forth. No more visualizing images. Beside me stood Susan looking like she used to in our thirties! Her hair, shoulder-length and full, so unlike the thin patches she once had due to cancer treatments. At seeing her like this, I knew I had made it all the way out.

"Let's say goodbye to your old self," she softly said as we started to lift from the room. With a gentle feeling in my heart, I asked God to protect my family and then bid a fond goodbye to the body I was wearing only moments before.

A glowing energy then came all around us. Before I knew it we were enveloped in this special light unlike anything I had seen before. As it fully embraced us, I felt Susan squeeze my hand again, and without any effort at all we began to reduce from the space we were in and appear in a new space. Confused about so much, I asked, "If I am dead, how am I able to see you?"

Susan laughed. "It's like this for many people," she said. "They assume when you die, you leave the body and therefore leave behind all that you love. But it's not that way at all."

I was comforted by the will I felt within her to help me through this confusion. As she talked further about life after death, I could feel myself warming up to the idea because it was Susan, not some minister saying I needed to be saved due to my sinful ways.

It wasn't that I didn't think God was real. I did. I just didn't think you came back as yourself once you died. Previously, I had made peace with the fact I never knew who or what I was before birth, so assumed I would go back to that state of presence once I died.

But why had Susan talked about taking me home? What did that mean? With that, I began seeing more and more of my surroundings. Slowly but surely the space we were in began to fill with objects of familiarity to me. It was bizarre, but things just appeared out of what seemed like thin air.

Then the most amazing thing happened. I realized we were standing in my home with the sun pouring through the windows. In the background the radio was playing as the sound of the sprinkler watering the yard came through. "How did I get here?" I asked.

"Here?" she asked back. "Where do you think you are?"

"I'm home," I said thinking that was a silly question.

"Well, you're halfway right," she said. "You are in your home but it's not the same home. This is the one you built when you went to sleep at night, trying to feel your way to the house and yard your heart most desired."

That really got me thinking! How many hours *had* I spent thinking about these things? I know I often felt myself daydreaming about them, wanting and hoping to make our home a joyful and attractive place for my family, but for many reasons, I was unable to piece it all together.

"How long has this been here?" I asked.

"Well," Susan said thinking about it for a minute, "it started appearing here about a month ago, which is how I knew your time was coming."

Fortunately, she had the wisdom to let me just feel this for a while and not try to explain it further. All I knew was I was no longer in my body, but I was in my home.

Eventually, she told me I had friends, many of them, waiting to see me. I was surprised because it sounded like a lot of folks had known I was inching my way closer and closer over the past month. Susan explained that's what happens to people who die from a disease. Slowly but surely their life force reconstructs itself on the other side, all the while bringing with them all that feels like home; all that is precious.

Susan's delight in seeing me agree to visit with old friends was obvious. Many people, she said, don't feel like seeing neighbors or friends for a while because they don't know what to say or do given that it's been a while.

My friend's hand was now feeling more and more like mine, or should I say my hand was feeling more and more like hers. Warm, whole, healthy. It wasn't the feeling of tingles anymore. In fact it felt like my entire body wasn't old or tired anymore, either. It felt warm and alive. (It was that realization that woke me up the rest of the way.)

Electricity is the compass of God. I know this now because I felt it piecing me back together. Inside each of us, we see ourselves as someone of joy, fun, determination, or even sadness. Outside, electricity pulls together those exact strands for us to perceive and experience as reality. Eventually, we witness exactly what it is we believe. I felt this revelation in my heart.

I now know, just as we have genes enabling us to see the colors of the rainbow, we have genes enabling us to see the spirit of love, only no one really talks about it so they're dormant.

This is why I've come to you today. I want to be the one person who *is* talking about it, convincing you to activate those genes in your body.

Your choice now is to go on living the way you have, and see the slow destruction of Earth as it engulfs itself through war and disregard for nature, or activate your mind and eyes by asking your brain to translate the sights of love and joy.

It's a tough journey if you give into the temptation of fear. Don't let it bring you down. Remember to teach your eyes to see the positive in life, and before you know, the sun's energy that used to scorch your world will soften, and you will embrace The Light as Jesus intended for all of us to do: to be together through love without the chariot of death taking us there.

MARCUS

To be belongin' to an Irish family *in England* in the 1820s could be, as ye might surmise for ye'self, a matter of a challenge. We have quick wits and bright dispositions, but when taunted, are beguiled to made quick of our tempers!

Enclaved in me room mindin' me own business, I heard a real ruckus outside. Once up to inquire, I found I was, in fact, in the middle of a dispute between me landlady and her portly husband. Right in front of me'self they fought as if I hadn't been there.

Refusin' to leave 'til I had the opportunity to hear for me'self what all the ruckus was about, I saw he had her by the throat and wasn't about to let go. He glared at me'self somethin' fierce, but then hid his eyes and crept off after lettin' her limp body drop.

God help me, I thought. *I'm livin' with a madman! What should I do? Where shall I go? I'm not educated. To start over again as a spindle maker would be near impossible in this culture of Irish disdain.*

Challenged to come up with a plan, I plowed through me things and found me holy crucifix. Takin' it to me heart, I heard inside me'self the directive to leave England and go back to me own people, in me own country, Ireland.

Oh, how I disliked that idea. Cryin' as I packed, I stole me'self a wee bit o' bread from me landlady's countertop and chose a hand cloth (which I had a particular fondness for over me years there) to wrap it in.

Still dirty and small, Blane was me home, so back to Ireland I went. Although black death had come 'round the village, most of me kin had survived. Life there was about horses. Mostly about breedin' and trainin' 'em. For me'self, horses were a pest. They demanded so much care. (It is so if ye own one.)

Back home I saw for me'self how few of me fellow countrymen could read or take direction without great help. To read, common folk had to watch those who could read and then piece together for themselves the sounds with the letters.

But noblemen of Irish descent were allowed to read only if they were capable of takin' direction easily. Because I had an aptitude to follow directions, I was given to readin' but if truth be told, it took great effort.

Ye might be askin' ye'self what gave me Irish nobility? When me da's family arrived on the shores of Scotland durin' one of the wars between the islands, it was assumed they were noble, for the words they used and the way they carried themselves lent it to be so.

Because the somewhat friendlier Scots reasoned they were of some finery, me da's family took that and made it their own. So strongly did they assume the position of finery that before me own precious da was born he was regarded by his neighbors and the church as a silver spoon baby; a baby whose future was assured of some distinction.

So long ago it was now I tell ye, but back then it added to a person's life a wee bit of fortune. Then why would a lad such as me'self leave such a fortunate life? Because I knew certain their story was ill-fated due to the immersion of the Irish comin' into Scotland as laborers. I knew certain me family would be exposed and did not want to be there when their house be looted, burned or worse.

Stubborn people rarely let go of a good story, however. But even as the Irish poured into Scottish ports makin' trade with the locals (tellin' their fibs and fables), the tale of me parent's heritage was unexpectedly *not* exposed, nor was it rotted. So there it is for ye to know. We were ordinary folk!

I tell me tale too long, I fear. So back to life in Blane. It was good for me'self, a lad of seventeen, because I was inquisitive and givin' to workin' hard. Before long, I was offered the position of instructor at a sort of farm for boys who would someday breed and tend horses for the finer folk.

These boys, it was widely known, would someday put Blane on the map among the prestigious landowners. But for these lads to make their way up in the horse tradin' industry, the sum of readin' and writin' would be important.

Me first year there I fell in love with the niece of the governin' family. I inquired about her on and off, but no one else made inquires on me behalf. So strange it seemed to be in love without so much as knowin' the flower's name.

Eventually, me wild Irish rose came to me'self on her own! Her horse had a bad nail in its hoof so with that as our meetin', we began our life of love. Her lips, more lovely than all the candlelight in all the windows, and her eyes so lively and yet so mellow, I knew straight away I wanted her to stay with me'self forever.

There are millions of stories like mine in Heaven, but mine, I fear, is only interestin' to me'self. But if ye care to know more, I commit to ye the followin': After we struck up a friendship and took to groomin' our horses together, we opened up to the worlds we could explore together. Hers was the wide world of wealth and privilege. Mine the lowly world of an instructor. What could I offer her?

Sorrow then overcame me'self. I stood apart from her in me heart for months on end. Not knowin' what was wrong, she came 'round on occasion but I had only emptiness for her inquiries. (Classless, I was.)

Lookin' to remedy me'self, I sought to teach me'self to read and even quote a few Bible verses. It was me one true love's wish that should we marry, we read Bible passages to our growin' family without great hardship. To that I applied me'self completely.

English and Scottish lassies are very much different from Irish lassies, I dare to tell. They are without the spark of life that gives the Irish their fancy. (In Ireland, if you are not with fancy, you are without the gift of lore.)

Me rose, Margaret, was with the gift beyond any other I had met before or since. She could sing a ballad or tell a tale that held the room or brought down the house.

A strong darlin' she was. Tall, too, for a girl, she held her ground. "Marcus," she would say lookin' directly in me eyes, "Go fetch me some water so I can toss it over ye head!" I would laugh so hard I nearly cried and even brought her up a cup or two through the years to see what she would do, but never did she dare to pour it over me'self knowin' I would risk a hand to her backside!

Alas, over fifty years later, I'm old and alone. Me darlin' Margaret went home through the bringin' of our fifth child into the world. In childbirth she was not so strong. Her heart, worn out, let go and there I was a man without the love of his life for the rest of his life.

I tell ye this because I need ye to know the more I fell in love with her, the more I knew we would be apart someday. It's like that with Jesus, our Heavenly Father. He wants us to know how to find our way home, so he takes one of the two of ye home before the other. That way, God willin', ye feel with all of yer heart yer direct passageway home.

Me passageway was with me rose, Margaret. With glory! As I lay dyin' on me bed, not movin' for hours, scarcely hearin' me grandbabies faint cries in the outer room, I knew in me heart I had somewhere better to go. After me final breath, me spirit left me body straight away. I sighed and strings that held me'self down sprung loose, freein' me'self to be on me way once more.

Margaret's name was all I could think of while liftin' from me body. It's as if it was comin' through me ears like a tune off a fiddler's string singin' "Margaret" to me'self, over and over again.

Strangers then approached and swore to me'self I was welcome! They greeted me with applause, which overtook me eyes. They said they were there to help me'self lift from me body and take me'self directly to Margaret because love *is* everlastin'.

Then I heard the roar of the oceans. It was incredible, I tell ye now! All the oceans breakin' into rhythm, together. Then at once, without so much as a blink of the eye, there came from the distance an ever increasin' white light beyond me ability to describe. This light was everythin' I ever loved or cherished, combined!

Suddenly, I drew into it without knowin' how I was movin'. At the speed of light I was comin' faster and faster into the realm of Heaven! Pulled long, but still me'self, I knew I was comin' into the realest place that ever was.

Carressin' me with joy, The Light itself picked me'self up and then put me'self back into me body but in this place I was young again. Life had not ended!

As I stood there with me new eyes and body, I knew me heart was not altered of anythin' good, only the sad and the pitiful. I could feel every worry and doubt I ever felt, every insecurity and frightenin' push, lift from me'self. I was whole again!

Lookin' and feelin' young again was proof enough to me God is real, but when the stirrin' of the wind took me eyes to the room beyond where I stood, I ran forward because there was me rose, Margaret!

She wore her grin of gladness and peace that always told me'self she knew deep within we were inseparable. Her eyes that sparkled with good cheer were still there, even in me earliest moments of redemption.

I long to tell ye more, but I tell ye more than I should already given the heart's ability to take in only so much. So as I leave ye, I ask that ye pray for yer heart to lead yer soul. It's a gift to be in love. But it's an even a greater gift to give love. Never deny givin' yer heart that opportunity.

For Margaret and me'self, I bid ye farewell and hope we'll meet again someday if our stars are to cross. Until then, know that I love ye, as I know ye love me. I feel it and thank ye deeply.

RALPHIE

Injuries happen, sure, but what about those you don't cause yourself? I was going down an elevator when suddenly it shot straight down. That plummeting feeling is all I remember now, because it happened in a split second.

But then, aware I should be hitting bottom at some point, I arrived in the sunlight. The brightest star in our universe delivered me out of my body and supported me as I flew up to be one within The Light.

How often does this happen? I thought. *It can't be happening all that often or surely I would have heard about it by now.* But there I was, like a ray of light, shooting directly into the sun.

Speed is relative. I wasn't wearing anything I could gage the speed with, but I'm quite sure I was traveling at least as fast as the speed of light. Stronger and stronger I felt The Light pull me up and into the clouds. From there, amazingly, I could still see the city streets and even the playgrounds with children. *How high will I go?* I wondered.

Lifting higher still, I worried if I went too high I wouldn't make it back into my body should the elevator somehow stop. But up I went until I could no longer see images on Earth I could recognize.

Where am I? I'm above the Earth, that's true, but is this a place? I wonder if this is where people go when they die. If that's true, don't they wear wings or something?

Once I reached the point of being so high I could no longer see the world I knew, I felt the chance to belong to a new world. What would make me feel that way? And what kind of new world would that be? Have others gone there too? If so, how did they get there? Were they pulled out of their bodies, too?

How funny it was to have the world below I loved so much become something I was being offered to leave behind. Whatever it was offering me a new world, I knew it had to know what was best because I could feel my life back there in danger, but not up here.

Suddenly, there was a jolt. It stopped. The elevator came to a complete stop. *How can that be? I wasn't even on Earth a second ago and now I'm in the elevator again and am perfectly fine.*

When the doors opened to the third floor I realized I had dropped almost fifteen floors without so much as a second in between. But in that time I had shot out of my body, made my way into the upper levels of Earth, and was rewarded with the promise of a new world.

Hold on a minute. Now you may think I died and came back in that elevator into the new world, but I'm here to tell you it's not like that. When you die you cross over and get together with your friends and family on the other side. What I had was a friendly one second out of body experience, but within that second I was shown and promised my life ahead.

There in the sun's light I saw and felt The Lord *is* Jesus Christ. It was proven to me because I asked to see him and there he was, walking with me and thousands of others like me. We all wanted to be a part of the Second Coming, so Jesus told us to be brave and know that when you choose him, you come home for brief moments to reinstate your health, and then come right back to continue with your life.

"But what about Christians who die?" I asked The Lord. He walked with me and let me see pictures of each of them being shown the road to everlasting life, over and over again until they choose for themselves to be born again exactly as themselves.

"Because," Jesus said, "they are more important to me than anything. Each human being is a precious gem. If even one is not here with me in their heart, I feel like a parent whose child is lost, and I come looking for them."

That must be sad, I thought. *Jesus has to come looking for us. Why don't we just know to look up and allow our eyes to float us into his Kingdom?*

Jesus answered that because most of his followers believe in his resurrection, they're able to feel their way up into the new world without having their souls rocket their way there through the spinning cycles of Earth's core of gravity mixed with love and light.

"Oh!" I said. "Is *that* what happened to me?" I asked smiling. "Spinning cycles of Earth's core of gravity mixed with love and light?"

"Yes," Jesus said as he smiled back tenderly. "You're a mildly retarded fifteen-year-old boy who is one of my special children. I have asked for you to come up here and be with me for a while so I can express into you the desire to be born again, but not with water on the brain. I need you to be born without the condition of hydrocephalus."

I knew I was challenged because I had a rough start as a baby, but no one ever told me I was mildly retarded. Actually, it was a great relief to hear so I no longer had to feel bad I couldn't memorize things like other kids could.

But to be born again? How would that occur? Jesus smiled at me with a grin I knew I had seen before. It was somehow that same grin my uncle wore years ago when he saw me after my ski accident and said, "Hey champ, what's with beating the rest of us down the hill?"

Included in that grin I saw how my uncle knew deep within I was a tender child who *had* to go through some rough times in order to toughen up a bit. He knew I had to learn to hold my own in order to gain strength for my future as a champion skier.

In Heaven, Jesus showed me, all things are possible. "When you were in your mother's womb," he said, "you were provided all that you needed except you were reluctant to come out when it was your time. You pushed down in a way that did not deliver you, but managed to put too much pressure on your skull.

"It's my need," Jesus continued, "for you to come back without reluctance. I need you to want to come free from your mother's womb knowing as you prepare to be born I will be with you the entire way.

"I will stay with you as you come through the birth canal, and I will hold tight to you as you come out into the Earth's structure of livability. I will be with you as you draw your first breath, and I will be with you as you first open your eyes.

"I wish, however, you would want to call me 'mommy', first. This I know will be funny to you later, but as a baby I need you to know deep within your mommy I am there. Can you do that for me, Ralphie?"

"Of course I can!" I assured Jesus.

He smiled back at me and then added, "One more thing, my son. I want you to also call me 'daddy', because when you look up into your father's eyes I want you to know I am deep within him, too. Can you do that for me, too, Ralphie?"

"No problem! I can't wait! When do we start?" I was overjoyed to feel that I was going to go back in time into my mother's belly and begin to hear "all is well with the world," so when it was my time to come out, I wouldn't be reluctant to be born.

Here goes....and then it happened! My arrow of light shot me back into my body, and from there into my mother's body. (The strand of light that tethered me to Earth also tethered me to my mother.)

There we were, exactly like before, only this time I was whole and healthy at birth. The doctor shot a look of happiness at both my parents and I shot a cry of joy at being free to live in the new world!

Jesus chose me to be born in his world, free of any retardation. Now I can do anything, I felt inside! But how long will it take until I catch up with myself in the elevator?

That's when I dropped back into my body on the third floor. Whole, healthy and ready to become the champion of my high school ski team. But first, I want to tell you when I went home that night, I felt something different inside. I looked at each of my parents differently this time.

What is it that's changed in them? I wondered. They look exactly the same but somehow seem different. In fact, I look exactly the same but somehow seem different, too. What is it?

Funny. I think something weird happened today in that elevator when I delivered newspapers to the top floor of the bank building, but now I can't recall what it was. Oh well, all I know is that it feels like it's going to be a great day!

JEANIE

Tonight's the night I'm going to make up with my husband, I remember thinking. He had gotten mad over the kids' toys and the amount of noise they were making before he stormed out of the house. Days later I thought sure he wasn't coming back, but I was wrong. Dead wrong.

After my first child was born I let myself go. I thought it was understandable but now I know I could have tried a little harder to get back my shape and vigor, but for some reason I just didn't feel like trying.

By the time Cory had had it with me, he divorced me in every way possible other than legally. Because we didn't have much money, we couldn't afford a lawyer let alone two rents, so in many ways we were stuck with one another.

Months rolled into years and little by little he hit me more and more often without me pressing charges, which I now know would have meant a very different outcome for all of us. But excuses are not good enough. I was as much at fault for being a victim as he was for being a bully.

Sometime after our third child was old enough to walk and talk, Cory got to picking on the kids rather than me. I'm ashamed to say sometimes I thought it was a relief. I could tell when he was in one of those moods, so when he grabbed at one of them instead of going for me, it sort of felt like I was escaping something.

Tommy, our oldest, had just turned five a few days earlier when he began banging on the drums we got for him for his birthday. I told him to go outside but in Cory's mood it didn't make a difference. He yelled a few choice words at Tommy and then left the house.

Days went by. That's when I decided Cory might not ever return. But then one afternoon while out back with the kids, he showed up going straight for Tommy. At first I froze, but a second later I flew to the ground on top of Tommy as Cory doubled up his fists and then really began to pound.

"Oh, God!" I pleaded, "Please make him stop." Eventually Tommy was able to run into the house to hide with his little brother and sister, as I sat on the ground in a ball taking all my husband's rage.

Lots of times on TV I had seen where a miracle took place and something made someone "see the light" but I didn't see a miracle coming for me. What I did see was Cory's fist. Coming square into my temple, he knocked me out, which was the last time I saw life as I knew it.

Shocked and maybe even bewildered at what he had done, he bent over and gave me a shake. Discovering I was dead, he gave me a kick and then calmly walked inside the house to call his friend for help.

While Cory was busy inside, I came-to but not like you might think. I came out of my body with the force of a woman in desperation. Although I knew I had died, I also knew I needed to protect the kids in case he was going to hurt them to cover up my death.

It all seemed painfully slow back then, but with my focus on the kids I finally got up. Walking was no good, I noticed, because I had no way to make my feet move. Eventually, I thought so hard about getting to the kids I just started moving there of my own determination.

By the time I made it inside he was still on the phone with his friend. Pals since junior high, they were always working on some deal to make money that most often wasn't legal. Convincing his friend to come over right away, he told him not to let anyone know and said he would explain more later.

Deep inside I knew Cory was up to no good. He looked at the kids like they were dirt. Looking at him made me feel sick but I had to do something so I sat down next to the boys and told them with all my might to take their little sister and go to the neighbor's house where she would hide them. I told them as loud and clear as I could, but neither seemed to hear me.

But a miracle was at hand! Their sister heard me! "Wait for me!" she cried as they headed out the door. God helped me to know somehow they would hear me and flee the house. "Thank you, God," was all I could think as she caught up to them outside as they headed next door.

Although panic caused me to think unclearly before, this time I wasn't going to let it keep me from protecting my kids. "Don't let Cory find them," I pleaded with God. "Please!" Just then I heard an ambulance coming down the street followed by a squad of police cars. My neighbor, my angel, heard my muffled screams and called for help.

Cory went to jail and the kids went into foster care. He made no attempt to see them or be involved in their lives, which is just as good, but it also meant they were without their grandma because she was too frightened to go up against her son, too.

After the kids were taken away, I wasn't sure where I should go or what I should do now that I was no longer in my body. I was lost. Eventually, one night I sat down next to my youngest as she slept and poured my heart out to God, praying for guidance for the first time ever in my life.

Asking God to make their lives better than mine, I heard inside I was being offered the opportunity to be a guiding light for them. That frightened me. What if I messed that up, too? They would have to pay for my mistakes all over again.

Rays of light then poured over me and Jesus came to me in person. It's not something I can describe to you without tears pouring down my cheeks because Jesus is so beautiful. He told me if I took on this responsibility, he would make ready a place for the kids and me so we could all be back together someday, laughing and playing like we were supposed to so long ago.

Then Jesus showered me with his grace. He gently explained it wasn't my fault I had been a neglectful mother because when

I was small, my mother simply poured all her fears into me. He said she was now deeply sorry and hoped I could forgive her.

To say the least, that came as an incredible surprise because my mother wore out her welcome everywhere she went. Never once had I heard her say she was sorry to anyone for anything. Jesus smiled at me and said she was ill minded, and asked if I might, for the sake of the children, forgive her. Instantly I felt my heart start to warm, and said, "Of course."

From there Jesus put out his hand for me to take. I was overjoyed at the feeling of being escorted into The Light. Nowhere had I ever seen anything like this place before. Having heard about a place they called Heaven in the movies, I never really thought it was real.

Coming into The Light was like coming through a sunlit doorway where all the love in the world is on the other side. It was beyond whatever you might think. Instantly I knew I must have been forgiven by my own children to have made it there.

"That's right," Jesus said. "Your children, each of them, has come to see me. Each has prayed I take good care of you, and you be their mother forever and never be apart from them. They each want you to be their guiding angel from Heaven."

I could hardly believe my ears. My children had never been to church. What did they know about Heaven or angels? At that, Jesus showed me a picture of my children at our neighbor's house. After she called the police, she knelt down on her knees and prayed to God to protect us. And because she did so quickly, a band of angels poured over me helping to release me from my body quickly enough to get inside and protect my babies.

Jesus then explained there were others, too, that had prayed for me to be loved and protected, which was how I began to change. It's like that. When you feel loved and protected, you feel like you can love and protect. At last I was ready to love and protect my children, and said yes to Jesus' offer!

I beg those of you reading this to ask for God's loving protection every day of your life. Never discount the power of prayer. Believe in God's hand coming out of thin air, and take that hand to allow your life to reshape itself into the beautiful life it was always supposed to have been.

It's sad but true when you don't believe in God you have to touch those things in life that are ungodly. But when you believe, you get to come into a world where all things are blessed and never taken for granted.

Be sure you tell your children about Jesus' love for them. It's important because as a parent you can't be there all the time, but Jesus can. He can help to support them in their times of indecision, which helps them make the right decisions.

Dreams are on Earth so you can connect with those of us on my side. If someone you love has died, see them in your mind's eye before you go to sleep and then ask to be with them overnight. In the morning, I promise you'll feel uplifted and refreshed in a way that will amaze you.

Chances are you know me. My name is Jeanie. I am a girl, a daughter, a woman, a wife, a mother, a daughter-in-law, and now even a grandmother. More importantly, I used to be you, if you think you're not good enough to lay down the law that every person in your life needs to treat you with respect. I am healed now and hope my words help heal you, too.

Someday we'll meet, I'm sure. I feel the joy in my heart hearing you accept that my words carry some wisdom.

DANNY

Coming back to life after dying on the operating table was not something I had thought about because I was only fourteen years old when my family had its accident. Because I was not wearing my seatbelt like I was supposed to, I shot from the car when it hit the embankment. Twice I remember thinking, *This is it*, but then something happened each time to keep me alive, so after I made it to the hospital I thought I was supposed to survive.

Better I back this up by starting at the beginning. I was an only child who lived for the thrill of going fast, no matter what it was. Skateboarding, snowboarding, biking, four-wheelers racing down mountainsides, they gave me the feeling I was more alive than all my other friends.

When I was four years old my folks bought me a kiddy car, the kind with a battery in it. It was okay but when I was seven, I installed our lawn mower's gasoline engine in it. My mom was mad and impressed at the same time. That's when I knew I had it made!

I awoke each morning of my life wondering what daredevil stunt I could do that day. While working it out in my head, I sometimes wondered about the odds I could actually die, but it never stopped me.

Because my mom and I had a close relationship, I knew we would never argue to the point of trouble. But then one day when I took off without letting her know where I was going, she got real mad. It wasn't like her to get upset over something so minor, so I started feeling maybe she wasn't well. But I soon got over it.

Eventually, stronger and stronger feelings about my mom's health kept popping in my mind. Before long I had to ask if she was okay. Once I finally did, she looked at me like I must have been psychic.

As it turned out, my mom had been having troubles with her menstrual cycles so she was facing a possible hysterectomy. I wasn't sure what all that meant back then, but did see in my dad's eyes that he held further concern beyond saying everything would be okay.

Sometime later my dad took me aside to say my mom did need to have the hysterectomy because she was ill. I thought that sounded like half the story so I pressed him for more. Eventually he told me the rest. It wasn't her menstrual cycles; she had cervical cancer. They just started with the hysterectomy story hoping they could cover up the rest for a while.

My ego was upset. I can say that now but back then I punished them for neglecting to treat me like an adult. I couldn't see they were trying to protect me. Even though they should have told me truth, I shouldn't have gotten so mad.

Once my mom's operation was complete, my dad took me in to see her. She looked okay as far as sitting and talking, but her eyes were different. Very different. When I asked how she was, they both agreed the operation went well but there was a waiting period before anyone could tell if they got it all.

Sadness came over me. All those years of having fun seemed so primary compared to the depth of my parents' concerns. Suddenly I felt like a kid who knew nothing. But in that frame of mind I sought solace by looking at my mom and mouthing the words, I love you.

She smiled and quietly mouthed back she loved me, too. It had been a long time since I told her and it felt good. For once I was doing something someone else needed, not just what I needed. That's when I think I turned the corner and decided it was time I started growing-up.

Little by little my mom's strength came back. Soon we all started laughing again and even making plans for our summer vacation, only this time we were not going to be back at the same old place. We were committed to doing something new and different.

While I was in the backseat of the car going on about camping ideas, my dad turned away from the wheel for a second to add something quick about mountain bears when he missed the turn and we careened off the road, landing the car on its side.

It was awful. I knew I was hurt because I could see my own blood on my hands and arms. But when I saw my dad's face smashed into the steering wheel and my mom's hands covering her face but not much else left of her body, it was all too real. My family had just died.

"Jesus, if you're real, I need your help. I can't get out. I need to get out!" I prayed over and over until I think I passed out. The next thing I recall was a paramedic pushing my seat back into position and extracting me.

Because my parents had already died, most of the efforts were in getting me out alive. While my dad's body looked okay, my mom's wasn't so it really, really upset me to see her like that. But the strange thing was, I was seeing them somehow from inside me. Not through my eyes, I noticed.

How is that possible? I wondered. *I'm hearing and seeing everything without opening my eyes.* I realized then I was having an out-of-body experience. I was up over my body, mostly dazed but definitely aware of my surroundings, able to pick up on what was happening.

They kept working on me, thumping on my chest. "He's got a pulse, but it's dropping," one said. After they got my pulse back, they put an oxygen mask on me and transported me to the hospital.

At the hospital I was awakened over and over by the staff. They kept calling my name, "Danny..." "DANNY!" It was torment knowing my folks were dead, yet these people wanted me to wake up. I wanted to be left alone. Couldn't they figure that out?

To my surprise they got me to open my eyes long enough to shine a light into them. I woke up somewhat though mostly drifted in and out. Because of the severity of my wounds, they prepped me for surgery, leaving me in a dazed state of relief from both my wounds and the horrible sadness I was suffering.

Refusing to participate in my survival, I started deciding when to let go and die: before the operation or after? Why put them through it all? That seemed kind of senseless. So I decided. I would not let them take me into O.R.

That's when I started to seizure. I railed against their futile efforts to hold me down with what seemed like superhuman strength, and even pushed one of the nurses to the ground. When I did, I guess I did with such a grip the staff smiled and agreed I was a fighter which would help in staying alive.

I can't win, I remember thinking. *What do they know about me? Who are they to make that kind of decision? Didn't they know my folks just died?* Just then I heard inside, "They know, Danny. They know and it's okay. It's me, Dad. I want you to listen to me and quit fighting them." I recall his firm words were as clear as if you had a phone to your ear with the best connection, ever.

"I don't want you to fight living, Danny. Your mother and I are alright now but you have to be strong. You're going to be okay if you try, but you have to try harder."

"Oh, Dad," I cried, "I can't. I don't want to go on. Please don't make me. I won't try harder. You can't force me back there without you and Mom."

My dad didn't realize it, but my mind was made up. He tried and tried a few more times but when the time came for me to go under, the anesthesia prepared my body for the escape I desperately wanted.

My mom made it to my side just as the operation started. I felt her hand on mine and heard her inside telling me everything was going to be all right. At one point she asked if I were sure I didn't want to be back in my body. I told her I was completely sure, and that was that. I flat-lined just like in the movies, which sent the room into a beehive of activity. But I was free! I had escaped out my nose.

As I floated, I saw the ceiling open up and then the brightest light that's ever been in all of existence came to me. Before I knew it, I was in it completely. It was a glowing, warm, watery and sensory-filled light. As I soaked it in, I felt my entire body reassemble into the real me.

Whereas before I knew I was smart and capable because my parents told me I was, I now felt the full assurance I was that and so much more. I began to feel I was amazing. With incredible ease I could hear, see, and feel things much more sharply and deeply than ever before. I knew this was what living was supposed to be.

I stood and absorbed every last drop being offered. It was as if I had been dunked into the light of liquid love, itself. As I gained strength and awareness, I noticed a sensation of speed associated with being in The Light. Incredibly, I moved at the speed of light, which gave me a feeling of exaltation unlike anything before.

Dancing inside is how it felt; like music was mending my heart and soul. I couldn't bear the joy of it almost, it was so wonderful. And then just when I thought it couldn't feel any better, I heard my mom calling to me, "Danny! We're here! Danny!" Looking ahead, I saw them both. There stood my mom and dad looking just as I had seen them that morning before the accident, only now their eyes were free of the look of concern over my mom's failing health.

They were whole and healed, too! Best of all, we were all together. They embraced me and said it was natural I should want to live, but also natural I should want to be with them, so my heart just followed them there. It was my heart, they said with love in their eyes that convinced them to allow me to be together with them in God's home for families.

"Jesus made it to each of us, Danny," my mother told me. "He's The Light, the one who stripped all our sins away, and saved all the good for us to return to. He built this place of love so we could find our way back to one another."

Jesus Christ was a son, a man, a carpenter, and a prophet. But, he was so much more, I thought as my mom talked. Inside me there was an electricity sharpening every feeling I had as she described what Jesus had done for us.

That's when my dad spoke, beaming with excitement. "I'm *so* proud of you," he said. "Your appearance here tells me you were allowed to come home young because you were ready. You have enough confidence and talent to push into the minds of other young people that they don't need to reach high speeds in life to feel the elation of love and fearlessness. They only need to visualize their older, greyer body coming off them every time they ask to see it lift."

"It's that simple?" I asked.

"Yes, Danny, it is. Crazy we never knew that over there, though."

So many people worry constantly about one thing or another. So many press their palms in prayer but don't ask to see their own healed mind and body. I prayed to Jesus for help when first I was in the car accident, and he answered my prayers. Now I'm here in the world of love and want to be of service to you.

Please know when you lie down at night and fall to sleep, you have the option to stay on the lower level where you are, or if you believe in the resurrection of Jesus, you get to climb the ladder of time and come into more love for your next body and mind. It's been prepared for you, for a long time. Why wouldn't you want it?

Please let me know if ever you need help making up your mind to do this work. I can sit by your side and assist you in making up your mind to be without fears or worries. It's a mental picture you first have to try to see.

I need you to believe in the power of love. It *is* medicine. See it as a field of light so bright and filled with electricity, everything it is, is love! It is consuming the darkness even as you think about it now. Good job!

Take my advice to heart. You are made of love, but you forgot and allowed fears to take over. Now get back into The Light and make fear exit your body like smoke out a chimney.

I'm tall now. All grown up. While I was too young to die, I wasn't too immature to be a leader in The Light, so The Lord allowed me access back through my friend, Lynn Scott. I'll take her word for it my words are going to make a big difference. I think her work will, too.

RAVEN

After my work ended with the railroad, I wanted to get another job to help make ends meet. My job there wasn't exactly high paying, but with benefits I earned enough to stay on the reservation with my own people and not go bankrupt like so many others.

Incredibly, one evening as I was whistling back to a bird in a far away tree, a squirrel came into the area where I was sitting. As it worked on some cones still attached to a twig, I offered it a few nuts I had thrown in my pocket after dinner.

Slowly the squirrel came near, but with caution. Then standing up on its haunches, it looked at me as if it were no longer concerned over my size whatsoever. *What a brave little creature you are my friend,* I thought, *stopping at nothing to get what you want. You have even given me something to think about.*

A while after the squirrel ate all the nuts, I tossed it a rare buffalo nickel, something I carried in my pocket to remind me of *the old ways.* What happened next will surprise you I'm sure, just as it did me: the squirrel sat on the coin and floated up!

Solitude, I thought to myself, *I'm making this up in my head and now even my eyes are in on the trick.* But even when I winked, squinted and rubbed my eyes, there it was: a squirrel on a coin, just inches off the ground!

How should I describe this to you? Most of you are a white audience, so nowhere in your history did your ancestors probably tell you to go wherever nature tells you to go. But I did. So I gave into the squirrel's picture of floating above the ground, and then offered it my thanks.

Resolute in my heart that this was a calling to return to *the old ways*, I picked up the coin after the squirrel jumped off and held it tight to my heart.

Sundown. That's when this all started. I had prayed to my elders to help me find my way to another job when the idea of feeding the squirrel came to me.

Refusing to believe I had come into madness, I sought my oldest living relative to talk with about this experience. After sitting on my uncle's floor for about an hour, practicing in my mind how to approach this conversation, I settled into a spirit of calmness that my uncle would not judge me. He would just listen and offer back words of wisdom.

Little by little I described the event. At no time did he show any emotion of distrust or fear. His listening was pure. When I concluded by telling him of my need to understand what message I should take from this was, he calmly spoke:

"You are my brother's son. When you were born you were given the name Raven because it was the song that played from your spirit. Your spirit carried the wisdom of Raven, rare and true. In your eyes I saw it and felt it as true.

"But when you were young and nothing came of your wisdom world, you gave back your wings. You saw few were taught in school about our nature spirits, so you left it behind where most leave theirs behind as well: inside.

"When I called to you as a young man inside my heart, I felt you but never did I hear you call back to me, inside mine. Oh well, someday, maybe, I hoped.

"After a long time working for the railroad, I heard you were ready to retire. I thought maybe then you would return to *the old ways* and come back to your spirit of wisdom.

"But nothing came to me from you. No pictures of you showed up for me depicting you were ready. No mention of my name came into my thoughts with your words attached. Still, I thought, maybe someday.

"Perhaps I had pushed too hard from my world of hope,

but when you called today to see me, my heart swelled like when I first saw you on the day you were born.

"Sundown. Wonderful. It means you were heard by Wisdom, itself. It means your words of prayer made it into the world where we all hope and pray together of a better place for all.

"After you saw the squirrel, you had eyes of knowing. You knew to watch it. You gave it the respect it needed to reveal something to you. And when you gave it some nuts, you spirited yourself with it and began the flow of the eternal passageway to wisdom.

"Clearly, the squirrel liked what it saw as it stood tall to examine you and your world. Some may say it saw a human with the likeness of a man, but what the squirrel took in was *the old ways*. It was moved to enlightenment at the site of you sharing that coin.

"Rowing a boat is an art. It takes practice to learn to reverse directions or change course in mid-stream.

"With that squirrel, it rose up and saw you reversing your tide of thought to go back to your nature ways, to *the old ways,* and forego thinking out every answer.

"Upon watching you watching it, the squirrel committed the gift of wisdom enlightenment, and awakened the particles of realization in the coin to feel God's ways on Earth.

"Stories like this are often forgotten but in the land where Christ once walked, where feeble minded men were healed and crippled men walked, it was because Christ stood up and saw in their hearts they believed in a God who would someday come to heal them.

"It has been told of Jesus Christ's resurrection whereby the particles in his body reversed the effects of Earth's sorrows, and restructured Christ into the mind and body of love.

"Healers know him. He is Jesus and he is love. You, Raven, are wisdom. You are one of the few who will hear and experience my story, and know it is not a tall tale.

"To thousands of humans, we walk with a sadness over our lands, torn apart by the white man's ways. But I tell you, the white man is now arching light and energy through their hands, too, just as our ancestors once did.

"Together our worlds of peace and love for Earth and nature will come back for all our families to share. All will inherit Mother Earth with Father Time connecting them. All will survive and thrive and work with the ways of peace."

After hearing my uncle's projections about my gift of wisdom, I knew my work as a messenger of nature's ways of peace and love had to be my next job–no, my calling.

When I went home that night the squirrel kept crossing my mind. Before I finish though, I need you to know nature has asked me to assure you though you can no longer see me because I died, I have come back to life inside and am now that messenger.

Softly, I came from my body that night as I stretched out on my couch watching TV, but mostly daydreaming of my day. As I thought about my friend the squirrel, the image of a beautiful black raven flew directly over me, and suddenly I came free from my body without so much as a heart attack or stroke.

Nature solved the problem long ago by providing a ladder of time for each of us to follow, and it carried me to the world of peace and love. Someday, those who buried my body will know I still wear a body, only now it is made from love.

People: We are each God in some form. Pray with all your hearts to hear one another inside and someday you, too, will release your mortal body and reveal Heaven has always been within you to see and feel for yourself. You just forgot which eyes to see through.

Eyes that forgive are the eyes that endure. I know that now, and hope you know it, too.

GRACE CATHERINE

It's been over ten years since I died in a car accident. We weren't coming out of the parking lot particularly fast, but as my dad turned left he sort of slowed down to make sure it was clear. That's when it happened. From out of nowhere, we were hit. Badly.

I don't remember much except the driver of the ambulance telling the radio dispatcher I was critical and never mind about getting a hold of my nearest relative. They would be taking me directly into surgery as soon as we got to the hospital.

Crying inside I remember sort of whimpering that my life was very, very fragile. It hurt to move even the tiniest muscles or try to feel my fingers or toes to acknowledge they were still attached.

Still crying inside, I took off my fear by praying. I know that sounds sort of strange to put it that way, but when you're in fear, it's like a blanket over you. When you pray, it removes the dark energy.

Softly, while I uttered a prayer to Jesus, I heard deep from within I wasn't going to die in the sense of being dead to the world, but I was going to leave this side of Earth where you are.

Backing this story up for a minute first, I do recall after the accident as they were getting me ready for the ride in the ambulance, the EMT said to my dad behind the driver's seat that I was quite a beautiful young lady. He smiled at both my dad and me. That's when I passed out into what now seems like oblivion.

The reason I am mentioning this is because my dad only had a second to look at me, but when he did, I felt him enter my heart in a way I had never felt before. I always knew he loved me, but this felt bigger than all the times before–times a million.

Sounds then began to take place. Increasingly they came. First a sort of whistling noise like when the wind passes through a crack in a windowsill. Then it increased into an almost thunderous sound whereby I was jolted out of my slumber.

Envisioning seeing the inside of the ambulance still, I was overtaken by what I saw: day lilies by the hundreds! Bouquets and bouquets of them abounded all over the room I was in. Tucked neatly in a bed, I could tell I was recovering from my accident, but this sight was incredible for anyone to see!

How can I explain to someone who hasn't seen a room completely filled from top to bottom with day lilies what it is like? The most amazing part, beyond them being there, was the scent. Perfume could never come close to a scent approximating this.

Instead of just lying there taking it all in with my eyes, my feet began to itch and then my scalp and finally my fingertips. It was all very peculiar, but in moving my hand to scratch the itch, I was forced to look at my body. It was electricity without the form of blood, tissues, and bones enveloping it.

What itched then if I didn't have blood, tissues or bones? I wondered about it for a minute until I saw my other hand (the one I scratched with) move like it was still encased with my old body.

What is happening to me? I thought. *Could part of me still be alive and part of me be dead?* Standing up I found I could move my arms and legs exactly as before, only this time they weren't laden with my "body."

Can I explain to you why I emphasize the word "body?" I never recall being very good at running or doing anything athletic. My coordination was always clumsy, at best. To be one with my body was not in the cards I knew from the beginning, so the peace I made with myself back then was to be smart, instead.

Exactly as you may think, I became smart! I worked hard at it, too. But don't get me wrong, it didn't feel like work in the hardship sense. It felt like a driving engine wanting to go further and further forward.

Excited with each new discovery in my world, I soon became a sort of little know-it-all to my friends and family. They laughed as I enthusiastically came out with all sorts of facts and figures about obscure little things, or even big charts sometimes to outline my point about something I wanted them to understand!

I wanted them to know what I knew so we could converse about it in detail, but that doesn't always work out. Sometimes information about sea creatures in the Mediterranean isn't enough to keep a dinner table conversation lively. Oh well, I'm having so much fun elaborating about my love for learning I have run off from my point.

Oh, yes. I was itching and scratching when I found my body had a form unlike anything I had seen before. I was made of light! The hand I used to scratch with was too, only it was a bit more embedded with cells that still looked normal.

When I saw and knew I wasn't where I had been before, I concluded I must be dead, and this is the afterlife.

Horrible car accident, I heard earlier, and now here it was again. Like a menace in my head, I kept hearing it. *Horrible car accident.* "S-T-O-P!" I heard my dad yell. And then everything did.

Like others who have crossed over, first you go through The Light where you are carried back to the part of Earth from where you came. There you get to see and recognize things familiar to you, even though you are different. So it was with me.

After I got up from bed and walked around a little I noticed a button on the wall to call for help. I pressed it and almost immediately a woman with dark red hair came to me. Without so much as saying a word, I clearly heard her in my head asking me to mind her by crawling back into bed while she went to get help.

Really? Who would she get? A minister? A distant relative? Just when I thought I couldn't be anymore surprised, my childhood pediatrician walked in. *He's here!* I thought. I wasn't sure I'd ever see him again, but here he was. He's my friend, I remember thinking. Just then, he sat on the bed next to me, patted my hand and said to me in my eyes, "Welcome!"

Oh, how that word makes such a difference. Welcome! It means they've been waiting for you and now you're there, at last. Warm words, health-filled words, they were. I beamed back at him how glad I was that he was there to welcome me.

"At last," he said in my mind, "you're awake!" What did he mean, at last? It wasn't something I dwelled on because he made light of it himself, but I did keep the thought in the back of my mind so I could ask someone about it later.

Coming for me also were a few more people I sort of recognized. Kids I had known as a child, but never knew what became of them. Two of them I found out (sisters), had been in a bad car accident, too. They grieved about it at times, they said, but knew their mother and father would join them one day soon. In the meantime, they were with their aunt, who was like a pretty princess, one confessed as she giggled.

Aunts aren't exactly like moms, they admitted, but they are family and that's what this place is all about. I never knew, I shared. They laughed and said no one really figures it out until they start looking around and notice more and more of their family is coming back into their life.

"Family," their aunt told me, "is all here." I didn't understand. "You see," she explained, "no one knows they've died until they've experienced a car accident or some tragedy, so for them the wake-up part means they get to see those of us who died before them. So we see one another because we know where we are. We're here, in Heaven!"

Still, it didn't make sense to me. We're all there?

What I now know is we are all occupying the same space, but only some of us can see some of us. While some on your side can see some of us on this side, unless you believe you can, you don't. And unless those of us on this side believe we can see those left behind, we don't.

Although it doesn't feel like it, I've been here a long time now. I've learned how to hear my parents (yes, my dad survived the crash) when they are talking to me, and to come around them at those times. Often they are just looking out into space or reading something that reminds them of our life together, but I stay near them knowing they will hear me someday in return.

I've given you a lot to think about, I'm sure. I want to be a part of the solution on Earth for those who are grieving deeply because they are apart from someone they love.

God is Jesus. He died for our sins and opened the doorway for us to go on living. If you believe this you get to go there too, but don't wait to die to get there. Start now by asking your heart to hear from those you love who have crossed over. They're waiting and hoping you'll open that door, you know.

My name is Grace Catherine. I came back to tell you this story so you will know when you die you aren't alone. You have millions of us on this side standing ready to help you awaken to your new world. Just ask for help and we will stir you awake with all our hearts and souls.

I'm Lynn Scott's friend. I hold her high in my heart for having allowed me to speak my peace on having a life that feels like Heaven even before you die. Aim for it! It will come for you!

RICHARD

The rent was due but I didn't know what I was going to do. I had to make my share of it or I'd be out for sure this time. Nothing personal, but from my perspective it felt very personal, all things considered.

It was early November which meant I would be really cold if I didn't come up with some way to cough up $250. That's a tidy sum when you're a student working nights at a laundromat, but at least it was quiet there so I could study.

Well anyway, I walked around town a while 'till I came up with the idea that if I faked a robbery at work, I could claim my money was stolen, too. Under those circumstances my housemates would have to cover me, I convinced myself. I could buy time.

Not that I liked being a liar, because I didn't, but I had to get the money somehow. Stupid thoughts and ideas kept running through my head, but the plan to fake a robbery kept coming back more and more like it was a good idea.

Funny, after a while it started to feel like this was a great idea. Getting money for something that never happened and even sympathy, too, how ingenious could you get? So I stole a little money. Who would know? Who would care? Of course in hindsight, I couldn't have been more wrong.

The next night I waited 'till I was there alone. Two minutes to closing seemed reasonable for someone who would be casing the place. So after destroying a few things in the back room, I came out and called the cops.

Sirens blaring, they showed up without any suspicion I was the one they would eventually book. Taking notes as I was telling my rehearsed story over and over, the cops seemed less concerned about the missing money than for my safety. They said a group of guys had been tailing people home from work late at night, robbing them, with one getting shot.

Suspicion grew over the following weeks as I had to keep retelling my story about a short guy with a gun, who had thrown me halfway across the room after he took the money. But since I wasn't battered or bruised at all, the police didn't buy my story after the first night. Eventually, they subjected me to a lie detector test, which I thought I could beat, but of course didn't.

So now, instead of just paying my share of the rent on time, or getting tossed out for not having it, I was being arrested and going to jail for real.

Better I tell you now than later, jail is nowhere anyone wants to land. While you may think it's a bed, a meal and a roof, it's a stinking hole where stinking men would just assume use you for a toilet.

The reason I tell you this is because if anyone wants to pretend the plan I hatched might have worked out, I'm here to tell you it *never* would have. I knew that from the beginning but didn't pay attention to the strong hit I had to quit while I was ahead.

In fact, just before I pretended to lock the doors at 11:00, I had a sick feeling in my stomach if I went through with this I would end up going to jail, or worse. Well, the worse part came true. While fighting it out in jail over a gambling debt, I got stabbed with a penknife. (Truly, a pen sharpened into a knife.)

My lung was stabbed pretty bad before the knife was removed. At that point I recall the feeling that this time, for real, I *was* being robbed—of my future.

Oh, God, what do I do if I die? I thought. I was a stupid, stumbling guy who wanted to make something out of my life by becoming a firefighter. But without better grades they wouldn't let me apply. Going to night school seemed like a good idea.

Cameras in the prison caught it all. I was carted off by my cell mate and made to look like I was asleep, so by the time the prison officials figured it out, I was long gone. L-o-n-g gone.

Elastic rubber bands. You know how they have that funny smell? Well that's what I first sensed while coming out of my body. Strange, eh? Why would I smell rubber bands considering my surroundings?

I rode the wave of smelling the rubber bands 'till I finally woke up to the realization I was over my body. Next, somehow, I was rowing a boat with my back turned to shore so I had to keep looking over my shoulders to see where I was going to land.

One thing was for sure: I was lost. Wouldn't you think by now I might have guessed that I had died? But while this was happening, it felt so much like a dream with its crazy images I didn't really piece it together.

Court came next. Elongated in a sort of stretched out way, I recall being sucked into a giant arena where those of us there had to stay until they called our names. Only then would they hear our cases.

How could this be? Could I really be in a huge court of law where the decision would be made about allowing me to exist, even if only in the afterlife? Just one short year ago I was a guy who wouldn't hurt a fly and now I had no idea what would unfold.

What if I wasn't a good enough guy to tip the scales to let me continue on? Could it be true I would be banished into exile if I didn't have enough good in me? (I was told if you're not doing enough good to get into Heaven, you go into a banishment period where you just "are" and that's it.)

Surrounded by people I had once trusted when I was young, I saw my old bicycle pal Timmy go up to the microphone and explain I had been the best pal a kid could have. Stumbling, he said, was just who I was. It wasn't Richard's fault, he kept saying. His parents never liked him much. So after the accident with the boat propeller, they hardly ever helped him when he would fall.

I saw and heard a parade of friends come to my defense. They argued while it was true I was up to no good that night, most of my life was about minding my own business and trying to be one of the guys and fit in. "What's the crime in that?" one asked the judges up front.

Acting sort of embarrassed by all this attention would have been my normal reaction in the past, but here, I was keen on getting them to hear everything they could that was decent about me.

How they kept coming–math teachers, football coaches and even my own grandmother. At last, I thought, someone who really loves me and will tell the judges about all the good in me.

But as I sat there and she smiled at me, she nodded to the questions asked and sort of said she didn't know or wasn't quite sure about the answers because I never spent time with her after I got older. Sure, when I was a little kid I wore a big grin on my face without expecting anything in return, but later on she didn't know if I stayed that kind of guy or not.

Stopping for only a few minutes between witnesses (I guess you'd call them), I swore to myself if I were allowed to continue living, I would be different. I would never be afraid to smile at someone or give compliments to people I knew or didn't know.

Lot's of laughter then broke out. I hadn't seen what happened so I asked the fellow next to me what happened. He said I had "dropped the ball of banishment" when I went into my mind and talked with the future about being abundant with my smiles.

What did that mean? "Dropped the ball of banishment?" And, for that matter, what was funny about it? I didn't get it.

How I worried about this. Was I going to go into exile or would they see something in me for the future worth saving? How would this be resolved? Any minute now my entire future would be decided. "Help me, God! Please?"

Softly then, beyond the arena, a beautiful golden white light came over me that spoke deeply and lovingly within my being. This band of light spoke tenderly but with such authority I knew it was Jesus.

HOME. I thought about it for a minute. *HOME.* Why was that word crossing my mind over and over again? *Home. HOME!*

That's why I kept hearing it! The golden white light was bringing me an invitation to come home.

Whatever I had done, thought, said, or didn't say didn't matter so long as I could come into that light and leave this *arena of the INDECISIVES*. That's who we were. We were the ones on Earth who refused to stand for anything important. We just existed as if life would always be there; as if we were entitled to it.

But now I know differently. I know we have to have a passion for something or else the dwindling starts. And as the degree of caring plummets, the wasting soon amasses.

I know because that's just where I was in my hours of indecision about whether to do the right thing or not. I could have cared less which way a coin would have landed had it been flipped regarding my future: tell a lie/don't tell a lie.

Because I care about you more than you could possibly know, I want you to believe in yourself as a vital human being. I can see the auras around those of you who read material about world affairs and things that matter vs. those who could care less about the planet and its plight.

I believe in the choices we make. I believe it's more important than you will ever know to always keep yourself in check by doing what matters to your heart; by doing what uplifts you.

I believe in Jesus Christ. My life right now is in spirit, on the side where you go when your time as a mortal has securely been closed. Truthfully, I doubt if I would have turned my life around had I not been caught by the authorities. In fact, I'm sure I had placed myself on the road to self-destruction and was going there one way or another.

Life now is about others more than self. It's the best way to make your world a place you want to be in. Now, I wait each day to be in service to someone on your side, and then go to them in their hour of need.

God goes wherever you go. That's my favorite thought these days. It's fun to know so you think twice about all you do. Don't worry about crazy thoughts, though. Just know, what you do is what you do for all mankind.

I was a young man wearing his immaturity too far into his twenties. Now I am a mature man who knows who he is and praises God that maturity and miracles come from the same source: Jesus Christ.

Great job bringing my message through to others, Lynn Scott. I know it's been a job hearing my tale, but it's true and unvarnished for those who might take from it some wisdom.

Thanks for your offer in helping me to make peace with myself and my past.

AMANA

It's happening to me, I feared. *I must be dying.* I was lying on the floor not moving yet trying to with all my might. *I haven't any way to call for help*, I remember thinking. *It's almost midnight, and none of my neighbors are around to hear me call.*

I was scared, but to tell you the truth I was also somewhat amazed. Though I had been there half an hour already, I didn't feel abandoned or alone the way I imagined I might if ever in that situation.

Buddy, my dog, was near. I was nearly lifeless by then, but nonetheless he stayed right next to me and kept me company. At times he sort of whimpered and even pawed at me, but then settled down when I opened one eye.

At first I resisted coming out of my body because of Buddy, I know now. But Buddy would have been okay because right there beside me was Eli, my husband who had died of pneumonia only months earlier.

Looking exactly as he did before, he held out his hand and together we opened the front door and left the house. It was hard to leave it behind since Buddy and all our family memories were there, but Eli told me there was more in store for me than I could ever imagine.

A long line of people I knew from throughout my life were there in front of us. It was a sight for sore eyes, I can assure you. *What a blessing,* I thought. *You leave one another for a while, but when it's your turn to release from your body, the ones you know and love come for you.*

It took me by surprise how many people were in this greeting line. So many I can't even begin to count. But they were there with smiles on their faces all warmed up and ready to help me release the past and greet the future.

Incredible events then began to unfold. As I stood there looking into each of their eyes, I saw the events putting us into each others lives. I felt the reasons we crossed paths and knew then none of these people came to me through happenstance or accident. Each of us had something important to share enabling the other to become a better person.

From the moment I started feeling these memories, the belief began to grow within me that I was chosen to be a conduit for anyone still in the physical world wanting help to become a better person.

Why we come together is for that exact reason, I knew. *But why can't we share our experiences from the other side?* I thought. That's when I saw my spiritual advisor and compass, Christ Jesus coming for me.

He was more than The Light, itself; he was LOVE in all its glory! To try to share with you how he felt is like trying to explain the way a new mother or father feels when first they hold their newborn baby. Nothing prepares you for this intense feeling.

Handing me a rose, Jesus said it was my turn to come back and be a special guide and friend for those who need assistance in becoming Christians so they can feel the road to salvation that keeps them alive, even after death.

He showed me my work as a worker of light–a rescue worker. His words were, "Please shower my hungry children with words of love so they can feed from the fountain of everlasting life."

I was crushed I never knew my Savior like this before. I wanted to run I was so ashamed. But he softened my feelings as he added, "I knew you would want to do this work because you know how hard it is to truly know The Lord when men and women don't talk about The Lord as love, as much as they do about the fear and shame associated with coming to The Lord."

He was right. Most of my life I was uplifted more by songs and poetry than rabbis or preachers. My heart ached many times to have services describing an afterlife of peace and love, but most described how sinful we are and how sorry we should be.

Love, Jesus told me, is his Father, his Mother and his Holy Spirit. He explained in every way love is *my* entire being, as well, and began to shower me with his love and acceptance, which was a warm, deep feeling of joy and gratitude. Heart and soul, I was free of fear!

Halos, Jesus showed me, are above all his children. Those who want to be with him, listen through the circle of love hovering above their heads, adjusting their minds to include the beauty of all mankind.

His words rang so true it felt as if my heart would spill over and I would cry forever with love. He *is* my heart, I felt. All I ever hungered for is in Jesus. He saw me as a child and kept me with him, awaiting this day when he would greet me personally to take me into his circle.

Christ then accepted my pledge to be an honored guest at his table. He provided for me a cup of wine and piece of bread just as I had received so often through communion. He accepted my heart as the heart of his own child, and then asked me to accept his own body and blood in my body and blood through the taking of his bread and wine.

Words in my heart were softly singing, "My Father, who art in Heaven..." He *is* my Father, I felt. He *is* my Father!

"Love is going to reposition you, Eli and Buddy," he said. "When you awaken from your fall on the floor, you may not have full memory of this event, but your heart will have the memory and will serve you with its wisdom."

"Am I really going back there?" I asked.

"Yes Amana," Jesus said. "You are now my eyes, my ears, my hands and my heart. You are my living bridge of Jews and Gentiles reaching across the waters for peace and brotherhood. You are my story of the resurrection and the return. I am coming back through millions like you, Amana. Will you be my angel on Earth?"

Having to part from Jesus was a difficult feeling to grasp. I had only just arrived and yet I was being told my gifts were needed back on the other side. *If this is what Jesus wishes,* I thought, *then of course this is what I will do.*

Love returned me back into my body that night beside Buddy. This time, however, it was with my heart repaired from the pain of losing my husband because I now know Eli comes to me whenever I call his name and together we can still be a couple.

Home is where the heart is. My heart is in our home where Eli and Buddy still share a life with me. I always knew Eli came around on occasion, and even saw Buddy's tale wagging as he looked up quite often, but now I can sense Eli when I relax and take my time to feel for him.

As I come toward my day of death on this side I regret nothing. I am not just Eli's wife or my children's mother, I am Amana, a woman of great strength, love and beauty. I am also wise, patient and forgiving. *I am Christ's child!*

My parting advice for each of you: live for today! This is the only day you *really* have. It's important to pour all your heart into it. That way, you will always have a great day.

ANTONY

Turning the corner too fast in my parent's SUV caused me to swerve out of control. It didn't feel like it was going to be that much of a problem but it sure turned out to be.

After the car turned and then rolled down the embankment, I walked around the grounds for a minute or two trying to get control of myself and the situation. Battered and bruised, I realized I had been in a bad car accident and needed immediate help.

Starting up the hill toward the road I noticed I wasn't moving. Breaking my arm was one thing, but that shouldn't have affected my legs. Swerving around the corner, I figured, must have made my balance crazy so I decided to sit down and rest.

After a while, I got to thinking about the car and how many times it rolled before it finally came to a stop. *Geez*, I thought as I looked at its condition, *it's smashed up pretty bad. I'm amazed I was able to get out.* That's when I realized I had absolutely no memory of getting out.

Looking in the car, I saw the remains of what was me. *Oh God*, I screamed to myself. *I'm there, trapped in the car. Oh God, oh God, oh God. How can I get help? Is it too late for help?*

After that I think I blanked out because I don't remember much except I was placed in an emergency room with what seemed like a hundred doctors and nurses tending to me.

None of them seems super concerned, I thought. *Wouldn't that be a good sign?* They were so businesslike as they called out and took orders. Me? I was panicked inside but couldn't help myself by calling out. It was like I was sealed-up inside hearing all of what was going on around me.

After a few minutes I sort of calmed down. They were preparing me for surgery when the first ER doc came over to me and tried to get me to talk. "What's your name?" he almost yelled into my ear. "Your name?" he repeated.

Startled, I remember giving a groan. He took that as a sign I could hear him and take direction, so took a hold of my hand as well as told me to write down my name.

Looking at him took all my strength. While he held the paper, I scribbled Antony. "Antony," he spoke loudly to me, "I need you to sign a consent form so we can take you into surgery. Your left lung is punctured and you have a broken arm. Additionally, you need stitches on your back and scalp. Do we have your permission to take you into surgery?"

Oh Christ, I thought. *My lung is punctured. Surgery. I guess it's not like they can fix it with a bandage.* Wiping my tears, a nurse told me not to worry because they see this sort of thing often, and the doctor is a really great surgeon and will have me fixed-up in a jiffy.

With that I scribbled my name on the consent form, checking the box they pointed at giving permission for my next of kin to be notified should I die.

Next of kin, my mom. Holy Mary, Mother of Christ. She'll fall apart if something happens to me. I have to make it through. That's all I could think of–making it through so my mom wouldn't have to live with the grief her only son made a horrible mistake by accidentally swerving off the road to his death.

After the papers were signed, I was rushed into the operating room and given an injection of something that gave me even more pain inside, but they didn't know because I couldn't talk. It burned and burned without any relief.

Struggling to get free, I saw the doctors yelling at the nurses to restrain me but by then it was too late. I had a seizure and came out of my body right there in surgery. It wasn't a feeling I can recall now (how I came out), I just know I was suddenly out.

Free from the pain, I was grateful I could finally get through to them that I needed to call my mom and tell her not to worry about the surgery, but they couldn't hear me.

Having to go to my mom myself was next. For some reason I knew I had to get to her before they did, so I pushed myself into thinking about her, so I could bring myself to her.

She had already collapsed. I saw my dad there on the phone taking instructions about coming to the hospital immediately, but he was clearly not hearing them. He was trying to get control of the situation so he could help my mom.

Black hole. That's the fear I had. I knew if I let go of feeling my mom I would go through the black hole. It was there with me since I left the hospital, over my left shoulder, but now it was tugging on me, trying to pull me through it.

"Not yet!" I yelled. "I'm not ready. I need my mom to feel me beside her, first. She needs me. Show me she knows I'm here." At that, she stopped looking at my dad who had hung up and was preparing them to go to the hospital.

"No," my mother said. "I'm not leaving. He's here. Antony is here. I feel him. I know they need me there, but I can't leave him here." Frustrated, my dad left for the hospital, knowing my mom would not leave when she said it like that. A deeply religious person, we all knew she was very kinetically joined to Jesus, Mary, and each of us.

"Oh God, Mom, I'm so sorry. I'm so sorry. I didn't mean to be such a dope. I just swerved and missed the curve. It wasn't like I was trying to be a wise guy or prove anything. I just missed the curve. Please know I love you, Dad and Sis, and would do anything to undo what I did."

From the look in her eyes I could tell she was thinking about something. It was working! The more I talked to her the more I could see at least some part of it was getting through.

Collapsing had been an autonomic response to hearing the news I was in the hospital after a bad accident. But by the time my dad held the phone aside trying to get her to come to, she had already died and come back—that quickly.

That's not something most people know about where you are. Nobody really knows about the number of times we die, and then get sent back by Christ. But it happens in a matter of a split second, all the time.

My mom, in those seconds across with Jesus, saw me in The Light and felt me holding her, asking her to carry on and not be afraid for me. I asked her to be strong for Dad and Sis, who would really need her given how their worlds would also be entirely different from now on.

After we hugged for a long while, I let her go but said it wouldn't be time that kept us apart, only the distance of disbelief. I told her anytime she needed me all she would have to do is say so in her heart, and I would hear her and be there without delay.

All this happened after I was out of my body in the hospital; after I gave permission for my surgery. Although I had warmed up to the idea they were going to help me, when the surgeon gave me the injection that burned, I came to again and then had the seizure.

After my dad returned from the hospital with the news I had died on the operating table, he buried himself in my mom's arms and cried for a long time. Once completely exhausted, he sat quietly trying to contemplate his next move which was about the inevitable funeral arrangements.

But as he sat in his stupor trying to think, I got through to him. I saw it! I saw his eyes move in my direction. I could tell he was hoping I would still somehow be a part of their lives.

"I will, Dad! I'll always be here! I'm still here now! Please believe I won't leave you, Mom and Sis. I'm here right now. Oh God, Dad. I love you. Can't you hear me? Can't you feel me? I'm right here!" At that I cried, too. Together we sat side by side on the bed and just listened to the air in the room, still with the exception of the old alarm clock by his bed.

My parents and sister made it through the funeral and mass, but I could tell they went in and out of their bodies most of the time. When they spaced out, it was much tougher to reach them or communicate. While you may think being out of the body means you're able to cross over and be where I am, it's not. It means you're vacant and your spirit exists over the Earth during those moments.

I was glad I went to the funeral even though it was hard. Many of my high school friends stood up and spoke, even the ones I never would have thought would do it because they were so private. It's funny how something so awful can bring out something so important in people. What I also learned is how many people on my side attend funerals on your side. They want to support their friends and loved ones as they close the door to their mortal life.

After the funeral I did a few things with my family but unless they call for me, I spend most of my time on this side working with newborns and old people who aren't sure where they are. It's amazing, because even a newborn has to be coaxed into breathing again just like someone who passes away from old age.

I love your ability to ask questions and then read my mind, Lynn Scott. Most of all I love the way you want to help others know we should mind our hearts. I hope this helps people to get out of their heads and start listening to their hearts because that's where *we* are.

Remember, when you hear someone has "lost" a loved one, it's not true. In truth, they are found. It's the grieving ones left behind who are lost.

Jump across to this side! Tell your mind to *"mind your heart."* It's easy. Simple as that. Never forget: *MIND YOUR HEART!*

ENZIO

Yesterday when the door to the boardroom closed it was something I'd wondered about for a long time: what would I do when I leave this place? Would I stick around New York or go overseas? It didn't matter to me much except for the fact I hadn't planned on being on my own at this point in life because I really thought I'd stay married, get old and die in this city.

Oh, well. It's a story. But it's not really a bad one–unless of course you want to know how a man comes to the point in life where he has everything but could care less. There are many people like me on Earth, it's true, but few of them die and then come back to tell their story. This one is mine.

My name is Enzio. I fell asleep one night over a cup of coffee laced with many pills. Although I wasn't sure I'd taken enough to kill myself, I had. Kind of a cruel joke on myself that I finally did something right.

Well, back to the story. I died but didn't really think I had. I awoke floating over myself. It was weird because it didn't seem like I was over myself–more like I was apart from myself. But, there I was, not in myself.

If you've ever felt like you were slipping in and out of yourself then you know what I'm talking about. But for you, you have the luxury of trying it on, the in-and-out part. For me, I was out, and there was no way back in.

Life had come and gone, but I was still here. How could that be? Who was I if I wasn't the man on the bed with the coffee cup and pills? Was I still Enzio? Would I know the answer somehow? It's odd but it crossed my mind, *who am I now?*

At that point a very disturbing humming noise began. It wasn't very subtle. In fact, it started to feel like the hard noise you hear when a train is coming too close for comfort. The noise was, however, enough to get me to stop drifting with my thoughts about *who am I now?* and begin focusing my attention on the sound and what it was.

And then it happened: the star. The greatest thing I've ever seen in all my life! How can I begin to describe it to a man or woman who hasn't seen their own star?

Who am I now? had triggered the room to recombine itself into a sort of avenue to the life I just had. Now, with the light of my star coming into my eyes, I knew my life wasn't wasted. I knew my life was the greatest gift I ever received, and the cause and effect of my life had pushed forward a few lives to the degree I could feel within my chest the pain of my overdose lifting off of me.

Who am I now? I thought again, and then it really took off! I sought the star by leaning forward into it, then saw it coming for me. I saw the rainbow of lights over and under the star commencing my life into a burst of sparkling white lights, until *I* burst into love from every sense of my being.

Climbing higher and higher, I could feel The Light itself coming into my temples, filling my eyes with the comfort that my life was a good life and my heart a good heart. *Thank you, God*, was all I could feel. *Thank you, God.*

Holding me in that space, The Lord then spoke to me in my temples: "Enzio, it's not your time. It's too soon. You have many more people to know."

No, it wasn't a voice like we hear when someone talks to us. This was a knowing from within that was easy and smooth. It was without seams. It felt like myself in how it knew me from beginning to end, but it was so much richer than myself in how it depicted the world and how many women and men I still needed to meet and know.

"Love. That is why you are here, Enzio. The world needs your love. It needs your heart. It needs your caring touch and words. Don't you know that? Didn't I promise you your life would be filled with love when you opened your heart to it?

"I saw you working late nights more and more, taking in more and more money. I wore your heart when you asked the future what it held for you. I saw you wonder if this life held any reason for you anymore.

"People need you, Enzio. My people. I am The Lord and my people are here on Earth looking for God in many places, not knowing if God really hears them or cares. I need you to be willing to look at your life through love–and come back to those who are willing to help tell the story that GOD IS LOVE."

Oh, God! I thought. *God needs me to look at my life. What will be shown? What will I see? What will God see?* I then started worrying about the many stupid things I had done, knowing when I did them I would care later but I didn't care enough at the time not to do them. What would God think? Would God hate me and realize a mistake had been made in seeking me out to be of help and value?

Let me go, I argued with The Light. *Let me go so I don't have to see myself looking at the maid without her clothes on.* I didn't know I would have to see that. How I hated to see myself taking advantage of my ability to peek into her room. I was so ashamed I could die.

Love then came over me without judgment. It was a calming feeling never taking me to task, just asking if I were truly repentant for taking advantage of my position as a superior so I could have subordinates in my home to watch.

How was I going to get out of this one? I wasn't a bad or awful man, but I didn't save anyone from their life of sorrow, either.

Stronger than my shame, The Lord then spoke to me in my heart, asking me again if I were repentant. I hung my head and breathed a sigh and said I was very, very sorry for my bad behavior, and should be punished. Love, God told me, was going to carry my sadness for me, but I had to want to invite love in for me to be free and move forward. Otherwise, I would stay here indefinitely.

(pause)

Cold. Why is it cold? Who is there? I couldn't see anyone but felt the presence of a beast or a bad energy. It was a grimy sort of feeling. I sensed it crept and crawled but never stood tall. How was I to make it through this?

Outcasts then started to come around me. As I stood there, more and more of them approached only they were more and more ugly and mangled, one after the other. Dirty and stinking, the stench was overpowering.

God help me, I thought. *This is the worst place I've ever been in. How did I land myself here?* Where was I? Falling. Falling was the feeling overcoming me as I looked out my eyes but without any real feeling of a body.

Strangers, hundreds of them, kept coming toward me. Sorting through them I saw their eyes. Each had the look of sorrow and shame, but no real remorse. They all had that sort of angry victim look altering on occasion into pitiful sorrow or shame. But none of them looked up. None.

That's when it hit me. When I previously announced to myself how horrible I had been by peeking into the maid's room, I realized my own shame brought me here; here, where all must come who believe in repentance to work out their guilt.

Free me from my guilt and shame, I squeamishly thought (more to myself than to anyone or anything else). After that I just remember being left alone.

Have you ever been alone? I mean, truly alone? No one or nothing even remotely near you? Sound, in itself, is company if you're alone. But without so much as the whisper of the wind, it's reality-negating.

Time, it seemed, was completely still now. I was not old or young, wise or naïve. I just was, or am. I wasn't sure. But I did know the soundless pitch of nothingness carried me to an anxious place within myself because it wasn't what I had expected. I felt sure if I killed myself I would be free of myself. But instead, I was alone *with* myself. Me. That's all there was.

How I worked my way from there to now is unreal. I suppose if you're interested I will tell you bits and pieces, but it's enough to say I had to imagine myself growing up inside without my attitude that the world owed me something. I had to imagine myself being grateful for small, insignificant things, because that's what matters later.

For instance: water. To whatever degree one can imagine something is valueless, that's about where I put water. I felt it just was. But it talks. Water talks. Not really in the language of verbs and nouns, but it has emotions and gives messages regarding its emotions.

Every drop is a gift. It's too hard on my heart right now to go deeper into this, but suffice it to say, I listened. *Water is forgiveness, itself. Water is the forgiveness we all need to stay alive.*

Join me now, will you, in thanking God for the plentiful glasses of water that have kept you warm? (Warm, meaning alive.) It's water that offers you life, you know. I offer you my cup of wisdom: never, ever take water for granted again, my friends.

Saturated in guilt for having so little insight into the strength of water's pattern of forgiveness, I troubled myself even more over how I took for granted the water's need before I took my life to have me look at it just once with love.

There in my coffee cup, swirling around, water. God offered me one last chance to begin my healing by feeling water's miraculous properties, but I was intent upon freeing myself by killing myself.

Time was not, nor was anything else other than "I." I was. It seemed unbelievable, yet no one or nothing else seemed to be. Uncanny then how weird thoughts come through a man's mind. Thoughts of how when I was little I used to love the hand that patted my back when I was crying. Papa. That's who it was who soothed me. My father. He needed to have me see him when he was dying, yet I couldn't make it there in time so just let his servants do their duty by taking care of him.

Why? Why was I such a jerk? How did I come to that place? Couldn't I have forgiven him for those things he did that made me mad? Was it really worth holding those things against him until he died?

I hesitate to shorten this but need to, so I'll just say when I thought of the quiet hand on my back that would pat me when I was small and in pain, I felt it once again. It was great, overpowering, in fact! Can you imagine? Suddenly after being alone for what felt like an eternity, a pat on my back brought me back to the world of love.

Sorrow then lifted completely off my back. I saw and felt the joy of my father looking into my eyes. He was there, truly there! It had been so long since we had been together, and now it was really happening. God *had* heard me when I said I needed to be saved.

At this point I offer to each of you reading this important, and wise, I must say, conclusion that had I asked my father when he was alive to be my friend, I think he would have asked me to be his friend too, but neither of us knew how to do this transition.

Can adults who still are immature in their hearts ever forgive their mothers and fathers for giving them grief? Can we live long enough to begin to mend our own minds when we have spent so much time making up our minds that our parents still owe us something; therefore, the world does, too?

What is the world coming to when it fills up with millions and millions of men and women just like me, thinking *they* suffered so others somehow owe them something? What we get are angry and insufferably selfish individuals. God help us.

Coming to you now through Lynn Scott, I want you to know my penance has been paid. I know my words and caring heart are ministering to you if any part of what I've been through matters in your life due to any similarity.

I love you. I know you don't know me by name, but I am you, and you, and you, and you. I am all of you who forgot to take the time to thank God for the daily gifts you received. I know you hear me in your hearts because I can feel a change in mine, which means you have guaranteed me a shot at redemption.

When Jesus comes for you he'll walk right up in person to let you know your place with him is ready. You'll know it because only he will come. He'll wear a robe of white and read to you the story of your life from his heart. He'll show you where you were wrong, but never, ever will you feel the shame or depths of despair I did because I didn't believe in him.

As I continue on my way toward that day when I was *supposed* to die on Earth, I am comforted in the knowledge that my father, who did die a natural death, is awaiting my presence to take me the rest of the way into The Light. While it was my father who brought me back from the abyss, and my father who will be with me as I go into my future life with God, it's my Father in Heaven, Jesus, with whom I travel now.

Great to get to know you! Enzio is my name and I'm an Italian American who wants you to know you are loved by God more than you will ever know—and so am I. That's who I am now: LOVE!

FREDRICK

In bed at night I used to look up and count the stars as they shot across the sky. I could see as many as a dozen some nights, but most of the time I only saw three or four before falling asleep. Tumbling through the sky I saw these stars as my nighttime companions.

By the time I was nine years old, I had learned the major constellations. Watching them move throughout the seasons, I would run to see their belts of light while examining their positions to gauge what came next. To see where they were was to know what came next. To a nine-year-old, this felt like God communicating with me.

I traveled most of the oceans on board Navy ships as an officer by the time I was in my forties. I loved my career and made it to lieutenant without much trouble. As an unmarried officer, I stood out because I could work longer hours and volunteer for assignments others might have to pass because of their families.

Living around the world was fun, I can guarantee you that. Most of all I loved learning about the various cultures: the words, the foods, the clothes, the traditions. Everywhere I went, people exuded a passion to keep their heritage alive.

Following my fiftieth birthday I had an encounter I was not really prepared for: my grandfather came to see me in my sleep, or should I say, near sleep. I had just gotten comfortable in bed after having read a little and was about to turn off the light when I saw him, Grandfather Reiner. It was a real surprise, as you might imagine.

There he was, big as life standing at the foot of my bed looking directly at me as if we had been in the middle of a conversation just moments before. Stunned, I tilted my head from side to side wondering if I was hallucinating, but nothing changed. There he was!

Finally, I asked myself if I had had too much to eat or drink that night, when he answered. "No Fredrick. You're fine. It's me, Grandfather Reiner."

Amazed he was speaking without ever moving his mouth, I realized he had said it all directly into my thoughts. It was as clear as if he had spoken aloud, only without any of the background noise. This was spectacular!

I was about to reply aloud when he asked me to answer him from inside. He insisted it was better communication because we could feel the words as well as hear them as they were being expressed.

And so through my thoughts I asked Grandfather if I had a dream that brought him here. He told me yes, many dreams, but that wasn't why he appeared before me tonight while I was still awake.

His belief, he said, is while I'm away at sea on my next assignment there will be a terrible accident where someone will be hurt or die. He said the next in command will see it as his own fault, but move the order of assignments to make it look like it was my fault.

I was confused. It didn't seem like my next in command would ever do such a thing. He was a true leader and never shirked his own responsibilities. But Grandfather then spoke sternly to me and approached me somewhat closer. "Ricky, you're my grandson. I need you to stop making excuses for what your next in command may or may not do. It's more important you listen to me and do as I say. Do you understand?"

"Yes, sir," I said.

"Good," he replied. "Now listen up and watch your step from this moment on."

For over an hour he told me how an admiral had moved a few ships north toward the Atlantic Seas where submarines were known to surface from the Soviet Union. He explained this maneuvering was a part of a spy operation. Eventually, he told me a blunder would be made and someone on board would be held responsible for the death of a shipmate.

I knew he meant business by both his tone as well as the depth of his inside information. In the end, I agreed not to take the next assignment, opting instead to insist on retirement.

I rested some more before asking any further questions. He was quiet as well. Soon after midnight though, he said it was time for him to leave, but never to forget he's always there looking out for me.

It was an event I never shared with anyone. Just as promised, I did as Grandfather Reiner asked. And just as he warned, there was an international incident involving a Soviet sub and one of our ships up north. *Terrible loss*, I remember thinking.

Lost lives are something we in the military have to get used to. Sadly, most officers must use both hands to count the number of close friends and comrades they have lost to war. For me, it was a silent suffering I preferred to keep to myself.

When I was eighty-eight years old in an old folks' retirement villa, I swallowed something down the wrong pipe and then ingested some of the debris I had thrown up. It lodged in my windpipe and within a moment's time I was out of my body.

Slowly it seemed I was coming to. Having jumped out of my body so fast might have made me think I could move quickly, but it wasn't like that at all. When first I was sitting next to myself I had to think and remind myself why I was there.

After a few moments it occurred to me I had thrown up and died, but still I was upset that an orderly or attendant hadn't come to check on me yet. But as I sat there thinking about the shoddy circumstances of my demise, something miraculous starting happening: I rose up from my sitting position as if I had no sense of gravity at all.

Coming up higher and higher, I could see myself below with only a bit of sorrow. The truth was, I was glad to be out of that feeble old body. But how is it I was going up? I wasn't working on it with my thoughts. Just then I heard the same exact voice I had heard so many years before: Grandfather Reiner!

Grand and tall as he was in his younger years, he appeared to me without any stern voice or direction of will. He just smiled and said, "Welcome, son!" His words filled me with a joy I cannot describe. Although I was his grandson, he always preferred to call me Ricky or son, depending on the day and circumstance.

Attending my Naval school graduation (in spirit) he said said was one of his proudest moments. He clapped so hard he was sure those in attendance could hear him! He said *his* parents must have heard him talk about that day fifty or sixty times.

His hand was on my shoulder. While we rose up higher and higher, and he talked of the wonderful days in my past, I could feel his heart. *It's true*, I thought. *While these are words that could be spoken, when he says them through his heart I can feel them.*

Oh God, I'm so glad to still be alive, I thought. Nothing had prepared me for the ghost of my grandfather that night, and nothing had prepared me for my return into spirit–but here I am!

Love was and is the only thing I know that matters. Of course, our careers and times of independence are important, too, but only those times when you touch someone else's heart does it make your life worth living.

After I left my body and went with my grandfather, I came into the brightest light you can imagine. It's so important to me you know about it, because when it's your time, just let go and float up with it. Let it lift you, and praise God it's your time.

Sadly, those who think they are important to the world of finances or medical science often stay too long. It's their egos that capture and keep them in a cage of will. Instead, they should welcome the day they become free. That's the day they get to chase rainbows and not feel important but feel free!

Salty old men such as myself know that when they die they will go back to the sea and become food for the tuna, but I never knew I would be able to return in spirit to give back the joy I have been gifted since coming home.

Enlist in the services if you want adventure. Become a biologist if you want to know Earth's secrets. But listen to your heart if you want to become a miracle person. I know that in every man, woman and child there is a thread of greatness—it is their calling—and nothing should ever stop them from fulfilling that greatness.

Have a great day, but never forget: Those who rise up in the morning and declare it's going to be a very good day, have it offered to them.

ALFRED

Eleven months before I died I had the feeling something was up, but I didn't know what. It was just a feeling of anticipation, but it just about drove me to distraction. I owned a construction company and kept very busy most of the time, but at that point, I decided it needed to close down.

Funny, looking back all the signs were there. But when you're in it day-to-day, you don't have the same vantage point so things don't connect. I just thought it seemed like a good idea to close down the business.

From my end of things it was a pretty small operation but a good one. I owned and operated it for fifteen years with a decent reputation for getting things done on time and within budget. After a while though, I lost interest in doing all the work myself so I subcontracted jobs.

Building had always been my trade. I woke up thinking about it and went to bed thinking about it. It was always there. But when the time came to start letting go of it, surprisingly I found myself thinking about retirement, instead.

I gardened some as a kid, but never really got into it as an adult. My folks had a real knack for it, with a garden the entire neighborhood envied, but it never seemed like fun or relaxation so it bewildered me why folks would choose that for a hobby. That is, until I started to think about what to do in my spare time.

Sometimes my wife Mary would ask me to do small projects for her around the house, like clean up the basement or something like that, but if I didn't have a hobby to occupy my time I knew I'd be driving her around town on most of her errands, which was not my idea of a relaxing time either.

Starting with the day I chose to tell my wife about retiring, she looked at me as though I had said I was going to take a ride on a rocket ship to the moon. "You, retire?" she laughed, "I never thought I'd live to see that day!" She was certainly surprised, but then she also started getting used to it, figuring out ways we could do things together.

It's not that I didn't like spending time with Mary, it's just I didn't want to ride around town looking at fabric, taking food to sick neighbors, and flowers to the church and hospital. That's not who I was and I wasn't going to suddenly change, that was for sure.

So gardening started to look like an idea I could really sink my teeth into. While she was tending to the house I could build a greenhouse and grow things. Who knew, maybe I could make some money on the side selling plants. Others have.

Then one day while out on a site I heard my name on the loudspeaker, "Alfred, you have a call." I stopped what I was doing and headed for the phone. Once there I heard my sister on the other end telling me our folks' place was for sale and did I want to buy it.

The old farm was left to my sister and me in their will, but now my sister's meddling husband decided it wasn't worth his time or effort so they'd sell their half to me unless I wanted to sell my half, too.

Working the numbers in my head quickly, I got the clear sense this was exactly what I needed: seventeen acres and a house I could use when it rained. Sure, it was in pretty bad shape, but still it was okay enough for me.

After I told my sister I would buy her out, I could almost hear her relief. She didn't say so but I think she wanted it to stay in the family. That made me real happy and between us, we were ready to see the place finally get fixed up.

As the months rolled by and business tapered down, I looked more and more to my new venture just miles down the road for ideas and found it had all sorts of potential. I saw it with a pumpkin patch in the fall, a manger at Christmas, an Easter egg hunt in the spring, and a vegetable stand in the summer.

I could see me keeping real busy and maybe even hiring some help. I was truly getting excited!

Soon after I caught a bad cold. *What dumb luck*, I thought. *Just as I'm getting ready to put down stakes for the greenhouse, I get sick.* Lots of folks were catching it, but for me it was real unusual.

Stronger and harder each day I tried to get my bones out of bed in the morning, but it seemed like I had weights attached to my body. Before long I couldn't get out of bed without help. My body was broken, I knew, but with the help of Mary's good cookin' I felt sure I'd be better soon.

But then a fever came and before I knew it, it overtook me. It shot up so bad I don't recall what I said or did those last few days. But I do recall at one point when I had to go to the toilet I fell down a flight of stairs all the way to the front door near the porch where my wife was sitting.

Frightened, she called the sheriff's office. They came out pretty quick but before they could get me back into bed I had a seizure. I had ruptured my spleen, and the power of the pain shot me clean out of my body.

I heard them calling my name over and over, "Alfred. Alfred!" But I never came to. It was over. And to tell you the truth, I was glad it was done. I do remember feeling bad about Mary because she caught that cold, too. To put this on top of it seemed unfair but that's the way it happened, like it or not.

While watching the older of the two deputies, I sensed my name being called again, "Alfred." But this time it wasn't my wife or the officers, it was somehow inside of me. *What could that be about? How could I be hearing my name without someone saying it?*

Looking around I saw nothing unusual until I spotted my childhood dog, Skippy, running for me. Anchors came flying off my feet, and suddenly I was running for him. His eyes were alive and his head up high. He was there and I was with him, no doubt about that.

I wasn't sure what to do next. I could tell Skippy wanted me to follow him, but then there was my wife to consider, sick and sad, with my body getting colder. Still, Skippy wasn't going to leave me alone so finally I let him lead me to what turned out to be an unusual spot.

Just outside our yard there had always been a sort of peculiar piece of land that backed up to our fence. It was a patch where nothing seemed to grow. No matter what we did to rake, water or fertilize it, it stayed bare. But now it was alive!

As we walked into its space, Skippy and I came into what seemed like a bright spotlight coming from everywhere, not just one place. As I stood with him staring at it, it started to feel like I was being given a dose of reality unlike anything before. Something more real than the land or the waters–the sky itself beckoned to us.

I had always been a man of the land. Not so much the water and never the sky. I think I only looked up into the night sky once or twice in all my life to follow a shooting star, and even then I didn't see the point since I knew it was going to burn away.

But now the sky itself was instructing me with love that it was my time to come home, and to go tell Mary and the officers thank you for their care and say goodbye.

I heard all this inside me just like before, but didn't know if it meant I should actually try to tell them goodbye or just wave goodbye. After thinking about it on my way back to the house, I noticed in Mary's eyes a dreamy sort of look telling me she was okay about me having to leave, and she'd be with me soon.

I love her, I remember thinking. She's the only woman I ever really loved, but I was never one to say so. I hoped she knew it. *I need her to feel it, but now it is too late*, I thought.

Just then I heard inside that it's never too late and to tell her. I heard I should put my hand on her shoulder and tell her everything I need to say.

Trembling, I sat beside her. Looking into her eyes I think I saw her for the first time. I mean, really saw her. She was the very same eleven-year-old girl I first saw at the state fair with my cousin many years before. I never knew a girl that age could be so beautiful, I thought at the time, and now felt it all over again.

"You're beautiful," I said as I put my hand on her shoulder. "I should have told you more often. You have given me all I could have hoped for and more than I probably deserved. I love you, Mary. Please forgive me for leaving you with this mess."

I dropped my hand and looked into her eyes to see if she had heard any of it. Because I was new at this, I wasn't sure. But now Skippy was on his way back to the spot where we had been so I knew my time was nearly up.

Holding her hand one last time, deep within I heard her telling me I was the one she loved more than anyone, and wasn't sure how to make it without me. We both cried and then sat in silence for a minute.

When the deputies came to tell her it was time to call the mortician, I saw Skippy making circles and barking like the time was *now*. So I let go of Mary's hand, again told her how much I loved her, and kissed her cheek one last time.

By now she was getting up to go with the officers. But in her haste to relay information to them about my personal effects, I noticed her eyes had already changed. She was not entirely the same. It was as if she had exited her body just like me.

Struggling with this was hard, but Skippy persisted in barking and making it seem like I had to get going. *Goodbye, Mary*, I told her deep from within my heart. I did not look back but kept my eyes on Skippy.

Soon I was in a fog-like place. Where the bright light once was, now a spirit energy existed. It was like mist but felt warm and comfortable. I was okay even though this wasn't normal. In fact, I recall thinking this is odd, even though it didn't feel odd.

Lessons then came to me in the mist. They weren't frightening or sad, just little pictures of when I was young and tormented over some decision or frustrated over something I thought I should have understood. I saw me handling it pretty good for a young guy, I thought. In fact, I was kind of proud of how much I took instead of pouring it out as blame or excuses.

Lengthy pictures then came flooding including Mary and me buying our house and me working construction. Nothing major, but in our everyday life I felt our home of love inside of me growing brick by brick and corner by corner. It was as if we had placed a sort of blueprint in the sky above with our wishes and prayers, and there it was unfolding on Earth for us to live in.

Beacons of light then started to flood me. I was awash in the sun's twilight energies telling me I was a good man and should come home. I wanted to go but couldn't believe what I was hearing. I was good. The truth is, I had always felt inferior but hid it most of the time. Never did I believe myself to be good. God was with me. I felt it!

Just then I felt a hand on my shoulder like when I put my hand on Mary's. I touched it with my other hand and looked up and there was Jesus Christ! He was my mother, my father, my wife and all my wonderful friends and neighbors. His face was love and in his eyes I could see each of them beaming back at me how proud of me they were. I cried just like when I was a child, only this time from relief, not sorrow. I felt like I had passed the biggest test ever, and God said I could come home.

Jesus saw me see them in his eyes. He also saw me see myself in his eyes, too. He counted on me, he said, to tell others he is the love inside all of us, and to know love is eternal.

I feared death once. Now I know it's as natural as blinking or falling asleep. You just never know when it's your time. But when you look back and see the pieces of your life coming together, you see why you did what you did. Without a doubt there is a knowing deep from within which lets you know your time is coming.

I got to be there when Mary came home. She was a natural at it–just sliding out of her body while she slept. Once I was sad that I never told her how much I loved her much, but after she was back in my arms you can be sure I told her a million times!

We're off on vacation now most of the time. Sometimes we look in on our relatives, but mostly we just want to spend time together and really feel the person we fell in love with. "It's our gift to God!" we like to say. "God brought us together and now we get to give back to God the love he saw within us to share."

As far as I know no man or woman has ever looked in a mirror and said, "Look, there's God!" But I hope you will, because hiding behind your eyes is the voice and love of God that was put into you at birth bringing life to your eyes.

Look into your eyes in the mirror knowing your garden is awaiting. Have you visited it today? If not, why not? Take time out each day and visualize what it would be like to walk in the Garden of Eden and see yourself there.

What I now know is that's where our renewed bodies come from. Each of us has a healed mind and a healed body awaiting us inside. These healed minds and bodies are relaxed and at ease, never fearing a thing. When you start imagining wearing your new self, you start the process of releasing your old self as the new self fills in.

I'm here in The Light now for any of you wanting to know why it's important to get your new body ready. God is Jesus, and one of these days very soon he is going to come over you with a light so bright you won't believe it. And then you'll be asked to come into it by freeing yourself from your old self. For those of you who know to look to Jesus for your soul's restoration, you'll find your new body waiting.

I hope I have been able to be of help and thank you for letting me be so, if I was.

Epilogue

Home
is where the heart is
on *both* sides of the veil.

Where is home for you?
God needs to know.

Talk with God.
Feel God's love.

It's alive and precious,
and calls to you by name!

3193246

Made in the USA